Y0-BDV-335

P. P. RUBENS

Paintings – Oilsketches – Drawings

29th June–30th September 1977

ANTWERP
ROYAL MUSEUM OF FINE ARTS

This Exhibition
under the High Patronage of
HIS MAJESTY BAUDOUIN
King of the Belgians
and patronized by
UNESCO *and* ICOM
is organized by
The City of Antwerp
The Ministry for Dutch Culture
and The Royal Museum of Fine Arts in Antwerp
to commemorate
the 4th Centennial of Rubens's Birth

Foreword

The occasion of this Exhibition, which owes its existence to harmonious co-operation between the Belgian State and the City of Antwerp, is the four hundredth anniversary of Rubens's birth, which falls on 28 June 1977.

At the outset it appeared a bold venture to organize the first great display of Rubens's works at a time when museums throughout the world are reacting against the unbridled enthusiasm for exhibitions which is threatening the physical condition of unreplaceable masterpieces belonging to the patrimony of European culture.

It was justly feared that many foreign museums would not be anxious to part with such priceless treasures as the paintings, oil sketches and drawings of Rubens, the most universal of artists. Moreover it was soon evident that other countries too wished to commemorate the four hundredth anniversary of his birth. Museums in Vienna, Cologne, London, Paris, Leningrad and Florence were planning exhibitions, less comprehensive than ours but nevertheless important. This international interest testifies to high appreciation of the art of the Flemish baroque painter whose work expressed in such a many-sided fashion the principal ideas of seventeenth-century Europe. The humanistic attitude to life, and the Counter-Reformation movement within the Roman church, were the chief sources of inspiration that governed his artistic vision.

The energy and enthusiasm with which the organizers of the exhibition have worked for the past three years have been crowned with success. No fewer than 109 paintings and sketches and 64 drawings have been assembled from various countries of Europe and overseas. Not all works by Rubens that lie close to our hearts could be brought to Antwerp. I have in mind, for instance, certain portraits of the Master's witty, modest and devoted first wife, Isabella Brant, his second wife Helena Fourment with her luxuriant beauty and love of life, and his charming daughter Clare Serena. I also remember the self-portrait in which he depicts himself as an old, tired man awaiting the approach of death.

The ideal exhibition can only exist in dreams; and, as the Antwerp poet Willem Elsschot put it, "dream and deed are divorced by laws and man-made difficulties." Many a canvas or panel could not be transported because of its size or condition. Many museums wanted to keep particular works so as to organize their own contribution to the Rubens celebrations. All the more gratitude is owed to those institutions and persons who, in an unforgettable gesture of fellowship, have parted with some of their most precious possessions for the purpose of this exhibition.

I would have liked to name here every single one of those who have helped in this way, but they are so numerous that I must refer readers to the list on another page. It is a source of rejoicing that so many have understood what Rubens means to our people. He was the "child of fortune" of the City on the Scheldt, who lived in a time of strife and social misery but who, whith his exceptional talent and knowledge, his amazing energy and strength of character, conquered the world not by force but by the magic of his art and the generosity of his disposition. His gifts and achievements are still alive in the minds of his fellow-countrymen, and even more in their hearts.

I therefore venture, on behalf of the people of Antwerp, to express profound and respectful thanks to His Majesty King Baudouin, who has graciously accorded his high patronage to this exhibition. Many are the representatives of our Royal House abroad who have exerted themselves to secure a favourable response from the directors of museums to the requests addressed to them by the College of Mayor and Aldermen of the City of Antwerp.

I cannot in this introduction name all those who have contributed in one way or another to the success of the exhibition. As far as the Municipality is concerned, however, I will mention here especially Mr. J. Van Elewijk and his successor Mrs. L. Detiège, Alderman for Cultural Affairs.

I would also recall that both Unesco and the International Council of Museums have been good enough to bestow their patronage on the exhibition.

Finally I would address a word of thanks to my colleague Mr. Defraigne, who in 1976, as Minister of Public Works, provided the credits necessary to make it possible, from a material point of view, for the Royal Museum in Antwerp to present this exhibition in the most advantageous conditions. The final result of everyone's conjoined efforts is seen in this great exhibition, which I hope will impress upon the visitor the miracle of Rubens's art — an achievement in which more is displayed than can ever be expounded by human wisdom or human speech.

R. DE BACKER-VAN OCKEN
Minister for Netherlands Culture
in the Belgian Government

Introduction

The Antwerp Municipality did not wish to leave uncommemorated the four hundredth anniversary of Rubens's birth, which falls on 28 June of this year. The outline programme for the commemorative exhibitions and other art manifestations, approved in principle by the College of Mayor and Aldermen on 25 January 1974, already envisaged as the "focus of attention" a major exhibition of Rubens's works, to be held in the Royal Fine Arts Museum.

There has not previously been such a comprehensive and systematically arranged exhibition as the present one, devoted entirely to Rubens's art and comprising finished paintings, oil sketches and drawings. Many of the master's works have of course been seen in earlier exhibitions such as *Flemish Art* in London (1953) and *The Age of Rubens* in Brussels (1965), and art lovers will also recall the fine collections of oil sketches and drawings shown respectively at Rotterdam in 1953-54 and in the Rubens House at Antwerp in 1956. Mention could also be made of several smaller Rubens exhibitions such as that held in London in 1950, which included paintings, oil sketches and drawings; but these were naturally less varied and comprehensive than the one I now have the honour to introduce.

For those who were concerned in its organization this exhibition certainly constituted a challenge, as its success was by no means a foregone conclusion. There can in fact be no such thing as an ideal Rubens exhibition, as the organizers were well aware; and it was clear from the beginning that many pictures could not be moved from their present location on account of their size or state of conservation, or because of the fragility of the panels on which they are painted.

The fact that other countries were also mounting Rubens exhibitions in 1977 might have constituted an additional problem, but it was solved to the satisfaction of all concerned thanks to the spirit of good understanding and co-operation of the foreign organizers. It should be noted with particular gratitude that as a general rule priority in this respect was given to Rubens's city of Antwerp.

That this exhibition has been organized in spite of the difficulties referred to and of inevitable disappointments is due first and foremost to the kind co-operation of so many museums and collectors. We are deeply conscious that it has been a sacrifice for them, especially in this anniversary year, to part with such priceless possessions. Some of these are works that are normally never lent, and we are profoundly grateful to those who have made exceptions to this rule in order to further the design of the City of Antwerp to confer international honour on Rubens by organizing this exhibition. The fact that His Majesty King Baudouin has graciously accorded his Royal Patronage to the exhibition, and that it is being held under the auspices of UNESCO and the International Council of Museums, constitutes an honour and a recommendation that we value most highly.

It is impossible to name here all the many persons who have contributed to the exhibition's success. First and foremost I would thank Mr. J. van Elewyck, formerly Alderman for Cultural Affairs of the City of Antwerp, for his personal contribution. Next come the members of the Exibitions Working Group, who designed the overall programme, after which smaller groups were set up for each separate exhibition, including this one. The task of supervising the whole complex of arrangements for the Rubens Year 1977, and of acting as a link and stimulus between the working groups and the College of Mayor and Aldermen, fell to the Co-ordination Committee aided by the Budget and Finance Working Group, whose role must certainly not be underrated. The Public Relations Working Group has ensured wide publicity for the exhibition as well as for the whole commemorative programme.

The Municipality of Antwerp was aware from the beginning that this exhibition far exceeded the resources of the City alone, and that the co-operation of the Ministry for Netherlands Culture would be indispensable. We are therefore glad that representatives of that Department played an effective part from the outset in the activity of the Exhibitions Working Group and the Co-ordination Committee.

We extend our sincere thanks for the moral and financial support provided by Mrs. Rika De Backer-Van Ocken, Minister for Netherlands Culture in the Belgian Government. Thanks in part to her untiring good offices with her Government colleagues, especially MM. Defraigne and Olivier, successively Ministers of Public Works, the restoration and reorganisation of the Fine Arts Museum building that has been considered necessary for years was carried out, thus creating the opportunity to exhibit works lent for the occasion in conditions that display them to the best advantage. We also thank the relevant departments of the Ministry of Public Works for what they have achieved in this connection in a very short time.

The co-operation of the Ministry of Foreign Affairs, especially its Direction for Cultural Relations, has been particularly valuable in organizing the exhibition. We are also most grateful for the co-operation of Their Excellencies the Ambassadors in Brussels of countries that have sent works to be exhibited. Requests for help were never addressed in vain to Belgian Ambassadors in foreign countries and to their staff.

I express my thanks to the Commissariat-General for Tourism, the Belgian Radio and Television and the Postal services, which have done much to arouse interest, both in Belgium and far afield, for the Rubens Year 1977 and for this exhibition in particular.

I also thank the scientific and research staff and other personnel of the Royal Fine Arts Museum, and our own Municipal Directorates and Services. I would mention more particularly the First, Fourth and Sixth Directorate, the Services of Works and Tourism, the Information Department of the Secretariat, and the Secretariat of the Rubens Year 1977. The Education Service of the Fine Arts Museum and that of the Municipal Museums have already done much preparatory work and are ready to assume the responsibility of guiding the public.

Last but not least, I would mention three members of the Working Group concerned with this exhibition who have done their utmost for years to make this culmination of the Rubens celebrations a reality. These are Mrs. Gepts, Curator-in-Chief of the Fine Arts Museum, who had also to cope with the difficult problems connected with the restoration and reorganization of the Museum building; Professor Dr. Ir. R.-A. d'Hulst of Ghent University, whose advice as an outstanding expert on Rubens was sought at a very early stage and whose valuable co-operation has continued ever since; and M. Frans Baudouin, Curator of Museums of Art History, who took charge of the innumerable administrative and organizational aspects of the entreprise and was responsible for co-ordination. The energy, expertise and co-operative spirit of these three made it possible to overcome a host of difficulties.

In conclusion I express the hope that this exhibition, which has come about thanks to the co-operation of so many helpers, may contribute to a better knowledge of Rubens's work, and that the many visitors will find it a source of rare enjoyment and artistic pleasure.

LEONA DETIÈGE
Alderman for Culture and
Environment of the City of Antwerp

Explanatory Note by the Working Committee

The purpose of the Working Committee for this Exhibition has been to give as clear and many-sided a picture of Rubens's work as possible. Works have been chosen from all the various genres which the Master cultivated, and we have endeavoured to illustrate the development of his style at different periods.

The exhibition includes paintings, oil sketches and drawings, many of which have never, or very seldom, been shown before. With a few exceptions they are all from museums or private collections in foreign countries. We did not feel justified in asking for the loan of pictures that can be viewed in the Rubens rooms of the Royal Museum of Fine Arts or in other museums and churches at a relatively short distance from the exhibition.

Naturally we did not always succeed in obtaining the loan of paintings, sketches or drawings that we wished to put on show. There can be no such thing as an ideal exhibition, and many of Rubens's masterpieces are dispersed in museums all over the world. We express our especial thanks to the private collectors and curators of museums who have entrusted so many valuable works to us. We well understand the reasons that have made loans impossible in some cases. We are greatly obliged to the Ambassadors and other members of the Belgian diplomatic service who have facilitated our task by their active co-operation and have thus made a big contribution to the success of the exhibition.

It is no simple task to compile a catalogue which meets scientific demands and at the same time fulfils its principal function of providing the public with a readable guide. Our chief aim has been to achieve clarity and simplicity of arrangement. A short general account of Rubens's life and work has been prefaced to the catalogue proper, which consists of two parts dealing with paintings and oil sketches on the one hand and drawings on the other, corresponding to the division of the exhibition itself. The works within each group are listed chronologically.

The catalogue entries give a short description of the subject of the work in question, the date and circumstances of its origin and the purpose for which it was intended. The bibliography indicates the names of art historians who have made a basic contribution to the knowledge and understanding of each work. Data concerning provenance show how the course of history and especially the tastes of individual collectors have determined the present whereabouts of each item. To avoid needless repetition, the entries for oil sketches that belong to a connected series are prefaced by a short account of the nature and origin of the project for which they were designed.

The catalogue was compiled, in collaboration with Professor R.-A. d'Hulst, by members of the scientific staff of the Royal Museum of Fine Arts, in particular Dr. A. Monballieu, senior officer, Mr. J. Vervaet, assistant, Mrs. Y. Morel and Mr. E. Vandamme. Mr. Marc Vandenven was responsible for co-ordinating the editorial texts. The English translation is by Mr. P.S. Falla.

Dr. G. GEPTS   Prof. Dr. Ir. R.-A. D'HULST   F. BAUDOUIN

The organizors of this exhibition express their gratitude to

HER MAJESTY JULIANA QUEEN OF THE NETHERLANDS,

for graciously granting the loan of a drawing by Rubens, and wish to offer their sincere thanks to the museumdirections, private collections and all those who, by their generous co-operation, made it possible to realise this exhibition:

Their Excellencies Mr. Kurt Farbowsky, Ambassador Extraordinary and plenipotentiary of Austria to Belgium; Mr. Lucien Lamoureux, C.P., Ambassador Extraordinary and plenipoteniary of Canada to Belgium; Mr. Anker Svart, Ambassador Extraordinary and plenipotentiary of Denmark to Belgium; Mr. Francis Louis Marie Hure, Ambassador Extraordinary and plenipotentiary of France to Belgium; Mr. Heinz Hoffmann, Ambassador Extraordinary and plenipotentiary of the Democratic Republic of Germany to Belgium; Mr. Peter Limbourg, Ambassador Extraordinary and plenipotentiary of the German Federal Republic to Belgium; Mr. Frank A. Coffey, Ambassador Extraordinary and plenipotentiary of Ireland to Belgium; Mr. Folco Trabalza, Ambassador Extraordinary and plenipotentiary of Italy to Belgium; Mr. M. Fischbach, Ambassador Extraordinary and plenipotentiary of Luxemburg to Belgium; Mr. Hugo Scheltema, Ambassador Extraordinary and plenipotentiary of the Netherlands to Belgium; Mr. Stanislaw Kociolek, Ambassador Extraordinary and plenipotentiary of Poland to Belgium; Mr. Serguei Kalistratovitch Romanovski, Ambassador Extraordinay and plenipotentiary of the Sovjet-Union to Belgium; Mr. Manuel Rodrigues de Almeida Goutinho, Ambassador Extraordinary and plenipotentiary of Portugal to Belgium; Mr. Nuno Aguirre De Carcer y Lopez de Sagredo, Ambassador Extraordinary and plenipotentiary of Spain to Belgium; Mr. Lars von Celsing, Ambassador Extraordinary and plenipotentiary of Sweden to Belgium; Mr. Auguste Hurni, Ambassador Extraordinary and plenipotentiary of Switserland to Belgium; Sir David Muirhead, KCMG, CVO, Ambassador Extraordinary and plenipotentiary of the United Kingdom to Belgium; Mrs. Anne Cox-Chambers, Ambassador Extraordinary and plenipotentiary of the United States of America to Belgium.

Their Excellencies Baron J. Papeians de Morchoven, Ambassador of Belgium to Austria; Mr. Ch. Kerremans, Ambassador of Belgium to Canada; Mr. J. Smets, Ambassador of Belgium to Denmark; Prince Werner de Merode, Ambassador of Belgium to France; Mr. R. Huybrecht, Ambassador of Belgium to the German Democratic Republic; Mr. Th. De Dobbeleer, Ambassador of Belgium to the Federal Republic of

Germany; Mr. A. De Vogelaere, Ambassador of Belgium to Ireland; Mr. A. Forthomme, Ambassador of Belgium to Italy; Mr. J. Dechamps, Ambassador of Belgium to Luxemburg; Mr. J. Lodewyck, Ambassador of Belgium to the Netherlands; Mr. F. Taelemans, Ambassador of Belgium to Poland; Mr. M. Wery, Ambassador of Belgium to Portugal; Mr. J. Herpin, Ambassador of Belgium to the Sovjet-Union; Mr. J. Verwilghen, Ambassador of Belgium to Spain; Miss E. Dever, Ambassador of Belgium to Sweden; Mr. G. Puttevils, Ambassador of Belgium to Switserland; Mr. R. Vaes, Ambassador of Belgium to the United Kingdom; Mr. W. Van Cauwenberg, Ambassador of Belgium to the United States of America.

Mr. M. Van Ussel, Ambassador, Permanent Representative of Belgium to the UNESCO; Count de Kerchove de Denterghem, Former Ambassador of Belgium to France.

AUSTRIA: Dr. Heribert R. Hutter, Direktion, Gemäldegalerie der Akademie der bildenden Künste, Vienna; WHR Prof. Dr. Walter Koschatsky, Wirkl. Hofrat, Direktor, Graphische Sammlung Albertina, Vienna; Herrn Dr. Erwin Mitsch, Graphische Sammlung Albertina, Vienna; WHR Dr. Friderike Klauner, Erster Direktor, Kunsthistorisches Museum, Vienna; Dr. Klaus Demus, Gemäldegalerie des Kunsthistorisches Museums, Vienna.

BELGIUM: André Leysen, Antwerp; Martin Wittek, Chief Director a.i., Koninklijke Bibliotheek Albert I, Brussels; Fr. Vanwijngaerden, Department Chief, Belgian Service for International Exchange, Koninklijke Bibliotheek Albert I, Brussels; Private Collection, Ghent; J. Sabbe-Vande Wiele, Kortrijk; Private Collection.

CANADA: Miss Jane Sutherland Boggs, Director, The National Gallery of Canada, Ottawa; Gyde Vanier Shepherd, Assistant Director, The National Gallery of Canada, Ottawa.

DENMARK: Dr. Jørn Rubow, Directeur, Statens Museum for Kunst, Copenhagen.

FRANCE: D. Ponneau, Chef de l'Inspection générale des Musées classés et contrôlés, Paris; J. Lacambre, Conservateur à l'Inspection générale des Musées classés et contrôlés, Paris; Mrs. Françoise Maison, Conservateur, Musée des Beaux-Arts, Arras; Paul Bazé, Conservateur, Musée Bonnat, Bayonne; M. Coutagne, Conservateur, Musées de Besançon; Mrs Françoise Soulier-François, Conservateur-Adjoint, Musées de Besançon; J.-M. Girault, Sénateur-Maire, Ville de Caen; Mme. F. Debaisieux, Conservateur, Musée des Beaux-Arts, Caen; M. Bertrand, Conservateur, Collection Mancel, Caen; P. Quarré, Conservateur en Chef, Musée des Beaux-Arts, Dijon; Mrs. M. Guillaume, Conservateur, Musée de Dijon, Palais des Etats de Bourgogne, Dijon; André Labarrère, Député-Maire, Ville de Pau; Ph. Comte, Conservateur, Musée des Beaux-Arts, Pau; Michel Laclotte, Conservateur en Chef, Département des Peintures du Musée du Louvre, Paris; J. Foucart, Conservateur, Musée du Louvre, Paris; M. Sérullaz, Conservateur en Chef, Cabinet des Dessins du Musée du Louvre, Paris; Mrs. A. Sérullaz, Conservateur, Cabinet des Dessins du Musée du Louvre, Paris; Mrs. A. Cacan de Bissy, Conservateur en Chef, Musée du Petit Palais, Paris; Carlos Van Hasselt, Directeur, Fondation Custodia, Institut Néerlandais, Paris; P. Quiniou, Conservateur des Musées Municipaux, Musée des Beaux-Arts, Quimper; François Bergot, Conservateur, Musée des Beaux-Arts, Rennes; J. Favière, Conservateur en Chef, Musées de Strasbourg; J.-D. Ludmann, Conservateur, Musée des Beaux-Arts, Strasbourg; A. Hardy, Conservateur, Musée des Beaux-Arts, Valenciennes.

GERMAN DEMOCRATIC REPUBLIC: Herr Rost, Verwaltungsdirektor, Staatliche Kunstsammlungen, Dresden; Prof. Dr. Manfred Bachmann, Generaldirektor, Gemäldegalerie Alte Meister der Staatliche Kunstsammlungen, Dresden; Dr. A. Mayer-Meintschel, Direktor, Gemäldegalerie Alte Meister der Staatliche Kunstsammlungen, Dresden; Werner Schmidt, Direktor, Kupferstich-kabinett der Staatliche Kunstsammlungen, Dresden; Frau Krüger, Sachbearbeiterin, Gemäldegalerie Alte Meister der Staatliche Kunstsammlungen, Dresden; H. Wiegand, Direktor, Museen der Stadt Gotha; Mrs. Ingeburg Neumeister, Stellv. d. Direktors der Museen der Stadt Gotha, und Leiter des Schlossmuseums, Gotha; Dr. G. Winkler, Direktor, Museum der bildenden Künste, Leipzig; Dr. L. Honigmann, Direktorin, Kunstsammlungen zu Weimar; G. Pommeranz-Liedtke, Direktor, Kunstsammlungen zu Weimar.

FEDERAL REPUBLIC OF GERMANY Prof. Dr. Stephan Waetzoldt, Generaldirektor, Staatliche Museen Preussischer Kulturbesitz, Berlin; Prof. Dr. Henning Bock, Direktor, Gemäldegalerie der Staatliche Museen Preussischer Kulturbesitz, Berlin; Prof. Dr. Matthias Winner, Direktor, Kupferstich-kabinett der Staatliche Museen Preussischer Kulturbesitz, Berlin; Dr. Rüdiger Klessman, Direktor, Herzog Anton Ulrich-Museum, Braunschweig; Prof. Dr. Erich Herzog, Direktor, Gemäldegalerie der Staatliche Kunstsammlungen, Kassel; Dr. F. Lahusen, Gemäldegalerie der Staatliche Kunstsammlungen, Kassel; Dr. G. Bott, Generaldirektor der Kölner Museen, Wallraf-Richartz-Museum, Cologne; Dr. Kurt Löcher, Wallraf-Richartz-Museum, Cologne; Dr. Wolf-Dieter Dube, Landeskonservator, Bayerische Staatsgemäldesammlungen, Munich; Prof. Dr. E. Steingräber, Generaldirektor, Bayerische Staatsgemäldesammlungen, Munich; Dr. Ulla Krempel, Oberkonservatorin, Bayerische Staatsgemäldesammlungen, Munich; Private Collection.

IRELAND: Sir Alfred Beit, Co. Wicklow.

ITALY: Onorevole Francesco Franchescini, Presidente, Comitato di Settore per i Beni Storici e Artistici; Prof. Salvatore Accardo, Direttore Generale delle Antichità e Belle Arti, Ministero della Pubblica Instruzione; Prof. Annio Giostra, Sindaco di Fermo; Prof. Dante Bernini, Soprintendente alle Gallerie e Opere d'Arte delle Marche, Urbino; Prof. Dott. Luciano Berti, Soprintendente per i beni artistici e storici per le Provincie di Firenze e Pistoia; Dott. Marco Chiarini, Direttore, Galleria Palatina, Palazzo Pitti, Florence; Dott. A. Lattarulo, Commissario del Commune di Firenze, Palazzo Vecchio, Florence; Dott. Ilaria Toesca Bertelli, Soprintendente per i beni artistici e storici per le Provincie di Brescia-Cremona-Mantova, Direttore, Museo del Palazzo Ducale, Mantova; Dott. Maria Brugnoli, Soprintendente alle Gallerie ed alle Opere d'Arte di Roma e del Lazio; Prof. Carlo Pietrangeli, Soprintendente ai Musei, Monumenti e Scavi del Commune di Roma; Dott. Giuseppina Magnanimi, Direttore, Galleria Nazionale d'Arte Antica, Palazzo Corsini, Rome; Drs. Luciana Ferrara Grassi, Direttore, Museo e Galleria Borghese, Rome.

LUXEMBURG: Artemis, S.A.

NETHERLANDS: Dr. Simon Levy, Chief Director, Rijksmuseum, Amsterdam; Dr. P.J.J. van Thiel, Director of Paintings, Rijksmuseum, Amsterdam; Dr. J.W. Niemeijer, Director, Rijksprentenkabinet van het Rijksmuseum, Amsterdam; B. Haak, Director, Amsterdams Historisch Museum; H.R. Hoetink, Director, Koninklijk Kabinet van Schilderijen 'Mauritshuis', The Hague, President of the International

Committee for International Art Exhibitions of ICOM; L. van Dorp, A.D.C. to H. Majesty the Queen of the Netherlands, Director, Koninklijk Huisarchief, The Hague; J.C. Ebbinge Wubben, Director, Museum Boymans-van Beuningen, Rotterdam; Dr. D. Hannema, Keeper, Stichting Willem Van Der Vorm, Rotterdam; Private collection, Wassenaar; Mr. C.P. van Eeghen, the Netherlands; Collection M.P.W.; Fa. H.D. Pfann, B.V.; Prof. Dr. J.Q. van Regteren Altena; Erven Dr. H.A. Wetzlar.

POLAND: Prof. Dr. Kazimierz Malinowski, Direktor, Muzeum Narodowe w Poznaniu, Poznan; Dr. Jan Baculewski, Director, Biblioteka Uniwersytecka w Warszawie, Warsaw; Mrs. Teresa Sulerzyska, Keeper, Department of Prints and Drawings, Biblioteka Uniwersytecka w Warszawie, Warsaw.

PORTUGAL: Joséde Azeredo Perdigâo, President, Fundaçâo Calouste Gulbenkian, Lisbon; Mrs. Maria Teresa Gomes Ferreira, Director, Museum Service, Fundaçâo Calouste Gulbenkian, Lisbon; Mrs. Maria Helena Suarez-Costa, Keeper, Fundaçâo Calouste Gulbenkian, Lisbon.

SOVJET-UNION: V.A. Popov, Minister for Cultural Affairs; Dr. B.B. Piotrovsky, Director, State Museum Ermitage, Leningrad; V. Suslov, Vice Director, State Museum Ermitage, Leningrad; I. Kouznetsov, Keeper, Dept. of Drawings and Prints, State Museum Ermitage, Leningrad; M. Varshavskaya, Keeper, State Museum Ermitage, Leningrad.

SPAIN: Excmo. Sr. Don José Ma. Socias Humbert, Alcade de Barcelona; Ilmo. Sr. Henand de la Sarte, Presidente de la Junta del Museo de la Virreina, Barcelona; Excmo. Don Juan de Contreras y Pérez de Ayala, Marqués de Lozoya, Presidente de la Real Academia de Bellas Artes de San Fernando, Madrid; Excmo. Sr. Don Xavier de Salas, Director, Museo del Prado, Madrid; Ilmo. Sr. Don Matias Diaz Padron, Conservador, Museo del Prado, Madrid; Da Rocio Arwaez, Archivista, Museo del Prado, Madrid; Ilmo. Sr. Don Carlos de Stuyck, Real Diputacion de San Andres de los Flamencos, Madrid.

SWEDEN: Bengt Dahlbäck, Director, Nationalmuseum, Stockholm; Mrs. Margareta Winqvist, Curator, Nationalmuseum, Stockholm; Bo Wennberg, Keeper, Department of Old Paintings and Sculptures of the Nationalmuseum, Stockholm.

SWITSERLAND: Dr. F. Baumann, Direktor, Kunsthaus Zürich, Stiftung Prof. Dr. L. Ruzicka, Zürich; Stiftung Sammlung E.G. Bührle, Zürich.

UNITED KINGDOM: Prof. Michael Jaffé, Director, The Fitzwilliam Museum, Cambridge; Duncan Robinson, Keeper, Department of Paintings and Drawings of The Fitzwilliam Museum, Cambridge; D.G. Banwell, Clerk to The Governors of Dulwich College, Picture Gallery, London; John Hayes, Director, National Portrait Gallery, London; Robin Gibson, Assistant Keeper, National Portrait Gallery, London; C.M. Kauffmann, Keeper, Department of Prints and Drawings and Paintings of the Victoria and Albert Museum, London; G. Duits, Director, Duits Limited, London; Prof. Kenneth Garlick, Keeper, Department of Western Art of the Ashmolean Museum, Oxford; Hugh Macandrew, Assistant Keeper, Department of Western Art of The Ashmolean Museum, Oxford; Private Collection.

UNITED STATES OF AMERICA: J. Patrice Marandel, Curator, Department of Earlier Painting and Sculpture of The Art Institute of Chicago, Chicago; Sherman E. Lee,

Director, The Cleveland Museum of Art, Cleveland; Mrs. Ann Tzeutschler Lurie, Associate Curator of Paintings, The Cleveland Museum of Art, Cleveland; Thomas Colt Jr, Director, The Dayton Art Institute, Dayton; Kenneth L. Mathis, Chief Curator, The Dayton Art Institute, Dayton; Frederick J. Cummings, Director, The Detroit Institute of Arts, Detroit; Ronals L. Winokur, Department of European Art of The Detroit Institute of Arts, Detroit; Robert W. Schlageter, Director, The Cummer Gallery of Art, Jacksonville; Samuel Sachs II, Director, The Minneapolis Institute of Arts, Minneapolis; Mrs. Marilyn Bjorklund, Registrar, The Minneapolis Institute of Arts, Minneapolis; Allan Shestack, Director, Yale University Art Gallery, New Haven; Fernande E. Ross, Museum Registrar and Curator of the Intra-University Loan Collection, Yale University Art Gallery, New Haven; Thomas Hoving, Director, The Metropolitan Museum of Art, New York; Anthony M. Clark, Chairman, Department of European Paintings of The Metropolitan Museum of Art, New York; Mrs. E.E. Gardner, Curator, Department of European Paintings of The Metropolitan Museum of Art, New York; Jacob Bean, Curator of Drawings, The Metropolitan Museum of Art, New York; Dr. George Szabo, Curator, Robert Lehman Collection, The Metropolitan Museum of Art, New York; Katharine Baetjer, Associate Curator, Department of European Paintings of The Metropolitan Museum of Art, New York; Marceline McKee, Assistant for Loans, The Metropolitan Museum of Art, New York; Moussa M. Domit, Director, The North Carolina Museum of Art, Raleigh; Mrs. Dorothy B. Rennie, The North Carolina Museum of Art, Raleigh; Robert B. Tonkin, Chief Curator, The John and Mable Ringling Museum of Art, Sarasota; Mrs. Elisabeth S. Telford, Registrar, The John and Mable Ringling Museum of Art, Sarasota; J. Carter Brown, Director, National Gallery of Art, Washington; Charles Parkhurst, Assistant Director, National Gallery of Art, Washington; George Heard Hamilton, Director, The Stirling and Francine Clark Art Institute, Williamstown; Richard L. Feigen & Co; Mr. & Mrs Eugene Victor Thaw; Private Collection – U.S.A.

Amadou Mahtar M'Bow, Director-general of the UNESCO; Makaminan Makagiansar, Vice Director-general for Culture and Communication of the UNESCO.

Dr. Jan Jelinek, President of the Executive Council of ICOM; Luis Monreal, Secretary General of ICOM; Dr. P. Cannon-Brookes, Secretary of the International Committee for International Art Exhibitions.

Prof. Dr. Müller Hofstede, Kunsthistorisches Institut der Universität Bonn, G.F.R.; Prof. E. Haverkamp Begemann, Dept. of the History of Art, Yale University, New Haven, U.S.A.; Prof. J. Rupert Martin, Chairman, Dept. of Art and Archaeology, Princeton University, Princeton, U.S.A.; Prof. Dr. Gert van der Osten, Cologne, G.F.R.; Prof. Paola della Pergola, Rome, Italy; Dott. Nolfo di Carpegna, Rome, Italy.

J. Van Elewyck, Member of the Belgian Parliament.

W. Debrock, Former Administrator-General, Ministry for Netherlands Culture; E. Grandry, Ambassador, Secretary-General at the Ministry for Foreign Affairs; E. Ceule, Administrative Director at the Ministry for Foreign Affairs.

R. Van Hauwermeiren, Consul General of Belgium in New York; E. Vanderlinden, Consul General of Belgium in Munich.

Miss Claire Kirschen, Counsellor, Embassy of Belgium in Paris; Chr. Fellens, Counsellor, Embassy of Belgium in London; C. Dewever, Firt Embassy Secretary, Embassy of Belgium in Rome; Mrs. G. De Ro, Attaché for Cultural Affairs, Embassy of Belgium in Madrid; A. De Buck, Attaché for Cultural Affairs, Embassy of Belgium in Bonn; A. Konovaloff, Attaché, Embassy of Belgium in Moscow.

A. Haulot, Commissioner-General; M. Six, Deputy Commissioner-General; J. Gyory, Chief of the News Service and Public Relations, their staff and the representatives of the Belgian National Tourist Office in foreign countries.

P. Van den Bussche, Director-General of the Belgische Radio en Televisie and his staff.

Dr. R. Sneyers, Director, Institut Royal du Patrimoine Artistique, Brussels, and his staff.

J. Van Landuyt, Administrative Secretary, Cultural Relations Service, Ministry for Foreign Affairs.

CO-ORDINATION COMMITTEE FOR THE RUBENS YEAR 1977

Mrs. L. Detiège, Alderman for Cultural Affairs of the City of Antwerp, President; Mrs. M. Van Cauwelaert, Alderman for City Properties of the City of Antwerp, Vice-President; Mrs. A. Stubbe, City Clerk; P. Thys, Permanent Representative, Province of Antwerp; L. Schevenhels, Administrator General, Ministry for Dutch Culture, Brussels; H. Jacobs, Director, 6th Direction, City of Antwerp; Mrs. A. Van Cauwelaert, Deputy Chief of Cabinet, Ministry for Dutch Culture, Brussels; Mrs. D. Verstraeten, Commissioner, Ministry for Dutch Culture, Brussels; J. Gaack, Former Inspector General; F. Baudouin, Keeper of the Art History Museums of the City of Antwerp, Secretary.

WORKING-GROUP EXHIBITIONS

Mrs. L. Detiège, Alderman for Cultural Affairs, President; Mrs. M. Van Cauwelaert, Alderman for City Properties, Vice-President; Mrs. A. Stubbe, City Clerk; Mrs. G. Gepts, Director, The Royal Museum of Fine Arts, Antwerp; L. Schevenhels, Administrator General, Ministry for Dutch Culture, Brussels; Prof. R.-A. d'Hulst, Professor at the University at Ghent; J. Van Ghyseghem, Chief Ingeneer-Director, Department for Municipal Works; H. Jacobs, Director, 6th Direction; P. Baudouin, Director, Cultural Department of the Province of Antwerp; L. Voet, Keeper, Museum Plantin-Moretus of the City of Antwerp; W. Van Nespen, Keeper, Archaeological Museums of the City of Antwerp; De Barsée, Chief of the Monuments Division, Department for Municipal Works; F. Baudouin, Keeper, Art History Museums of the City of Antwerp, Secretary.

WORKING-GROUP RUBENS EXHIBITION

Mrs. L. Detiège, Alderman for Cultural Affairs, President; Mrs. M. Van Cauwelaert, Alderman for City Properties, Vice-President; Mrs. A. Stubbe, City Clerk; Mrs. G. Gepts, Director, The Royal Museum of Fine Arts, Antwerp; L. Schevenhels, Administrator General Ministry for Dutch Culture, Brussels; Prof. R.-A. d'Hulst, Professor at the University at Ghent; H. Jacobs, Director, 6th Direction; J. Pauwels, Director, Service for Cultural Relations, Ministry for Foreign Affairs, Brussels; F. Baudouin, Keeper, Art History Museums of the City of Antwerp, Secretary.

WORKING-GROUP FINANCE AND BUDGET

Mrs. L. Detiège, Alderman for Cultural Affairs, President; R. Van Passen, Alderman for Finance; H. de Ruijter, Deputy City Clerk; H. Jacobs, Director, 6th Direction, City of Antwerp; J. Morrens, Director, 1st Direction, City of Antwerp; J. Weyns, Inspector, 6th Direction, City of Antwerp; J. Gaack, Former Inspector-General, City of Antwerp; F. Baudouin, Keeper, Art History Museums of the City of Antwerp, Secretary.

WORKING-GROUP PUBLIC RELATIONS, INFORMATION AND PROPAGANDA

Mrs. L. Detiège, Alderman for Cultural Affairs, President; Mrs. A. Stubbe, City Clerk; A. Van den Berghe, President of the Belgian Press Association, Section Antwerp-Limburg; H. Jacobs, Director, 6th Direction; L. Verhaert, Director, Tourist Office of the City of Antwerp; K. Aerts, Director, Belgian Radio – 3rd Program; L. Verwerft, Director, Tourist Federation of the Province of Antwerp; J. Brouwers, Department Chief, National Tourist Office of Belgium; J. Van Liempt, Production Chief, Cultural Department of the Belgian Television; J. Christiaens, Department Chief, Information Service to the Secretariat; F. Baudouin, Keeper, Art History Museums of the City of Antwerp, Secretary.

SOME NOTES ON RUBENS'S LIFE AND WORK

1577	Born on 28 June at Siegen, Westphalia, son of the Antwerp lawyer Jan Rubens and of Maria Pypelincx.
1598	Recorded as a Master Painter in St. Luke's Guild at Antwerp, having studied under Tobias Verhaegt, Adam van Noort and Otto van Veen.
1600-08	Rubens lives in Italy, in the service of the Duke of Mantua. Visits the great art centres of the peninsula and studies classical works and the Renaissance masters as well as contemporary Italian works. Paints several altarpieces and numerous portraits.
1603-04	First visit to Spain, on a diplomatic mission for the Duke of Mantua. There he admires numerous works by Titian, and copies some of them.
1608	Returns to Antwerp.
1609	Appointed court painter to the Archduke Albert and the Infanta Isabella. Marries Isabella, daughter of Jan Brant, an Antwerp lawyer and humanist.
1609-10	Paints *The Adoration of the Magi* for the Antwerp magistrature.
1609-21	Paints several important altarpieces for churches in and around Antwerp, including *The Raising of the Cross* (1610-11) for St. Walburga's and *The Deposition* (1611-14) for Our Lady's church, both in Antwerp.
1617	Designs cartoons for *The History of Decius Mus*, his first tapestry series.
1620	Designs ceiling paintings for the Jesuit church in Antwerp.
1622-23	Designs cartoons for *The History of the Emperor Constantine*, a tapestry series commissioned by Louis XIII of France.
1622-25	Executes a series of pictures for the Long Gallery in the Palais du Luxembourg in Paris, commissioned by the Queen Mother of France and depicting *The Life of Marie de' Medici*.
1626	Death of Isabella Brant.
1627-28	Designs cartoons for *The Triumph of the Eucharist*, a set of tapestries commissioned by the Archduchess Isabella.
1628	Second diplomatic mission to Spain, where he again admires Titian's works and copies some of them.
1629-30	Diplomatic mission to England. Knighted by Charles I.

1630	Marries Helena, daughter of Daniel Fourment, an Antwerp dealer in silks and tapestries.
1630-32	Designs cartoons for a series of tapestries depicting *The Life of Achilles*.
1630-34	Paints for Charles I of England the ceiling decorations for the Banqueting House, Whitehall, London. Also paints in these years some of his finest altarpieces.
1634-35	Designs and directs the decoration of the city of Antwerp for the State Entry of the Cardinal Infante Ferdinand.
1635	Acquires the Château de Steen at Elewijt near Vilvoorde, where he paints many landscapes.
1636-38	Designs decorative paintings for the Torre de la Parada, King Philip IV's hunting lodge near Madrid.
1640	Dies on 30 May in his home at Antwerp.

The Artist and His Wife, Isabella Brant, in the Honeysuckle Bower, Alte Pinakothek, Munich

The Descent from the Cross, Cathedral, ·Antwerp

The Adoration of the Magi, St. Johns-church, Malines

Susann Fourment, National Gallery, London

Peter Paul Rubens and his Work

Max Rooses, to whom Rubens studies are so deeply indebted, wrote in the introduction to his monograph on the great artist, published in 1903: "His creative spirit was so indefatigable and his power so inexhaustible that it would be hopeless to attempt to discuss everything he produced, and, even confining oneself to the minimum, one would risk wearying the reader with an excess of subject-matter." These words are still true today, indeed more so than ever. Since the beginning of the century patient and exact research has added so many items to the catalogue of Rubens's works, and so much new information of every kind has accumulated from all sides, that it is no longer within the power of any single critic to furnish what could be called a thorough study of his life and art. This short introduction can only have the modest aim of providing the reader with some facts and ideas that may help to improve his knowledge of the Master.

Peter Paul Rubens was born on 28 June 1577. He was not an infant prodigy. True, he displayed a rich and promising talent at an early age, but he did not spring into instant fame in the same way as the youthful Van Dyck some years later. His craftsmanship developed slowly, but this was not due to indolence. From the outset his work was marked by rapid perception and accurate execution, but with remarkable self-discipline he laid the foundations of his technique in a methodical and gradual manner.

It may be doubted whether Rubens learned much from his first master, Tobias Verhaegt, to whom he was probably apprenticed for family reasons. In any case he soon moved to Adam van Noort's studio, where he stayed at least four years before finally attaching himself to Otto van Veen, one of the most prominent Antwerp painters. A man of taste as well as learning, Van Veen belonged to the group of 'Romanists' who had made the traditional journey to Italy and whose painting was imbued with Renaissance humanism. Van Veen's own pictures were not of the first flight, being serious and rather dull, but he was well fitted to introduce his pupil to the technique of composition and to stimulate his interest in the intellectual aspects of the artist's profession.

In 1598, after seven or eight years' apprenticeship, Rubens was registered as a Master Painter in St. Luke's Guild at Antwerp. Although thus entitled to open his own studio he remained with Van Veen, probably because he was already planning an educational tour of Italy, which attracted him as it had so many of his elders and contemporaries. No doubt his master, who had himself made the journey, encouraged Rubens to undertake it; moreover the artist's father had spent seven years in Italy and his eldest brother Jan Baptist had died there. Rubens set out in 1600, shortly before his twenty-third birthday. He was better equipped for the journey than most young artists of his day, not only because of his talent but because he spoke Italian, was a Latin scholar and was familiar with the principal authors of antiquity. It was not surprising, therefore, that within a few months of his arrival in Italy the Duke of Mantua, Vincenzo Gonzaga, invited Rubens to enter his service. He remained for eight years at the court of this ambitious and dissolute prince, a patron of arts and letters who made up for his faults by a genuine appreciation of beauty.

Rubens's duties at Mantua included copying famous paintings and portraits of attractive ladies, and also designing court festivities. Not least among the incidental advantages was the opportunity to visit other parts of Italy. Rubens made two long stays in Rome, visited Venice more than once, became thoroughly acquainted with Florence and Genoa and got to know other art centres near Mantua such as Milan, Verona, Padua, Pisa, Lucca and Parma. Few painters acquired a comparable knowledge of the wealth of art treasures in the peninsula. Rubens worked indefatigably, recording his impressions in drawings that he kept in portfolios for later use. He became an expert on Roman antiquities – gems, statues, sarcophagi and the Palatine ruins. Every feature of the Italian Renaissance excited his curiosity. The young Rubens admired the splendour of Venetian painting: the luxuriant colours of Veronese, the vivid rhetoric and drama of Tintoretto, but above all Titian's strong, flowing line, his powerful imagination and masterly sense of form, which Rubens studied with ever-growing admiration as time went on. He saw Michelangelo's amazing Medici tombs in Florence and his Sixtine Chapel in Rome, and never forgot the imposing nudes of the Italian master. While in Rome he spent hours contemplating Raphael's magical compositions in the Vatican Stanze and the Villa Farnesina. He was also strongly impressed by the works of Mantegna, Correggio, Raphael and Titian in the Duke of Mantua's collection, and retained a lifelong memory of the Palazzo del Tè, the summer palace that Giulio Romano built for the Duke and adorned with his own imaginative and vigorous frescoes.

Rubens also encoutered the works of his great contemporaries south of the Alps. He was captivated by Elsheimer's intense yet balanced vision and admired the skill and repose of Cigoli's altarpieces, while his Flemish feeling for nature was attracted by Caravaggio's emphatic realism. In Annibale Carracci's Galleria Farnese in Rome he not only found a new and magnificent decorative system, full of brightness and strength, but also a synthesis of all the great painting of sixteenth-century Italy: Raphael's echoes of classical beauty, the revelations of Michelangelo and the achievements of North Italian and especially Venetian artists. All these found a place in Rubens's art, skilled as he was in assimilating the work of others and subjecting it to his own artistic vision. Especially in his early years, but also later, he drew inspiration from models that he had before his eyes either as originals or in the form of copies by himself. Naturally the Flemish artistic patrimony, and not least the painting of Pieter Bruegel, also played a large part in inspiring his work.

Rubens's visits to other parts of Italy, and also to Madrid in 1603, gave him an opportunity to meet other patrons and to carry out commissions for them in so far as his obligations to the Duke allowed. Thus he painted portraits of Spanish grandees and altarpieces for the Roman churches of Santa Croce in Gerusalemme and Santa Maria in Vallicella, as well as for the Oratorian church at Fermo and the Jesuits' church at Genoa, where he also painted several portraits of the nobility. The Duke of Mantua commissioned three large paintings for the Jesuit church in that city.

In the autumn of 1608 Rubens received news in Rome that his mother was gravely ill. He set out at once for Antwerp, but when he arrived she was already dead. There is no doubt that when he left

Italy he intended to return there, but in fact he never again saw the country to which he had become so attached. For the time being, various circumstances combined to keep him in the Netherlands. The Twelve-Years' Truce of 1609 brought peace to the land for the first time in over forty years, and after the devastation of war there was immense scope for artists, as churches and secular buildings had to be restored and redecorated. The Archduke Albert and the Infanta Isabella, Regents of the Southern Netherlands, pressed Rubens to enter their service and offered attractive conditions, e.g. they allowed him to go on painting at Antwerp and did not require him to move to Brussels where the court was. Finally, and this was perhaps the decisive factor, Rubens fell in love with the eighteen-year-old Isabella Brant. The couple married in 1609, some weeks after Rubens was appointed court painter: he celebrated the event with a magnificent double portrait, now at Munich. Three children were born of the marriage. In 1610 Rubens bought an early sixteenth-century house to which he added a studio in Genoese style, adorned with classical sculpture and inscriptions from Roman literature.

As Rubens had foreseen, this proved to be a golden age for art at Antwerp. The city had lost much of its political and economic power during the long years of war, but its cultural life was still vigorous and many-sided. Besides Rubens, many other talented painters helped to give it fresh impetus: Jan Breughel, with whom he was closely associated, Adriaen Brouwer, whom he greatly admired, the masterly animal painters Frans Snijders and Paul de Vos, the somewhat younger Jacob Jordaens, who was to paint robust, impetuous scenes of popular Flemish life, and the lyrical Van Dyck, who was Rubens's assistant at an early stage of his brilliant career.

Rubens's fame had preceded him from Italy, and he was entrusted with important commissions directly after his return. One of these, for the Hall of State in the Antwerp town hall, was *The Adoration of the Magi*, a subject to which he reverted on several occasions. Abraham Janssens painted *Scaldis et Antverpia* (The Scheldt and Antwerp) to decorate the same apartment, and we may assume that both works were ordered in connection with the negotiations that were held there and led to the Twelve-Years' Truce in the war with Spain. Most of Rubens's commissions, however, were for altarpieces, which he painted for the cathedral and the principal old and new churches in Antwerp as well as for Brussels, Mechlin and Ghent. Rubens in fact painted more altarpieces in the decade after his return from Italy than in any other period of his life. The first of these were *The Adoration of the Shepherds* and *The Glorification of the Eucharist*, both now in St. Paul's at Antwerp. Much more important works, however, are *The Raising of the Cross* (1610-11) and *The Deposition* (1611-14), one painted for St. Walburga's and the other commissioned by the Arquebusiers' Guild for their altar in the cathedral. The Catholic revival known as the Counter-Reformation encouraged frequent depiction of the crucified Redeemer: the tragedy of the expiring Saviour, true God and true man, gradually supplanted the appealing scene of the Virgin and Child. In *The Raising of the Cross* Rubens created a new physical type of Christ, triumphant in suffering, an athlete wrestling with death. Many variants of this type can be found in the artist's later work. The triptych also contains many reminiscences of Italy. The diagonal composition recalls the style of Tintoretto, and both he and Caravaggio can be recognized in the strong contrasts of light and shade; the colouring is suggestive of some Venetian masters, and the stalwart executioners resemble certain of Michelangelo's figures.

In contrast to this vehement bravura piece, in which Rubens seems to parade all his new-found powers, *The Deposition* is marked by sobriety of execution, rhythmical composition and a colour-scheme in harmony with Flemish tradition. Compared with the models of Cigoli and Daniele da Volterra that can be discerned in it, the work is both more realistic and more attuned to sentiment. In this picture, which established Rubens's reputation as the foremost religious painter of his age, the emotional intensity of the Baroque period found full expression for the first time.

In the years following his return from Italy Rubens also painted numerous mythological pieces, not of course for churches but as decoration for guildhalls or aristocratic dwellings. In such works antique divinities were used to symbolize moral principles, thus satisfying his patrons' taste for humanistic lore and also their genuine Christian faith. Typical instances in Rubens's work are the delicate compositions *Venus, Ceres, Bacchus and Cupid* and *Jupiter and Callisto*, the luxuriant *Juno and Argus* and the powerful, impressive *Prometheus Bound*.

Rubens soon became so famous that, besides orders from his countrymen, foreign commissions flowed in from every direction: the King of France (Louis XIII), the Prince of Wales (the future Charles I), German princes, Spanish and Bavarian noblemen, Italian churchmen and Genoese bankers came to him for religious and mythological pictures as well as portraits and allegorical, historical or hunting scenes. In addition to his painting he was famous as a collector and connoisseur, and corresponded with experts and prominent people throughout Europe.

Attention has often been drawn to the matchless vigour of Rubens's imagination and the varied and complicated forms and actions that he sketched with apparently effortless rapidity, with what Bellori called his *furia del pennello*. This aspect of his skill is attested by the enormous range and quantity of his work, but it would be very far from the truth to suppose that it was one long improvisation. The many drawings and oil sketches that have survived show how thoughtfully he went to work and how he experimented repeatedly to find the best solution. At the same time, however much we admire the beauty and variety of these preliminary works, we must not forget that they always played a subordinate role and were not an end in themselves: they were preparations for the final work, and were designed to make it as perfect as possible.

At an early stage Rubens systematically organized the activity of his studio with its many artists, and in this way he was able considerably to increase its output. In about 1617 he was given the opportunity to make full use of the apparatus he had created: a group of Genoese noblemen ordered designs for a series of tapestries on *The History of Decius Mus*, a Roman consul in the fourth century B.C. who is said to have devoted himself to death to secure victory for his armies in a battle against the Latins. This was the first of the many cyclic commissions that were in future to make the chief call on Rubens's powers and win him the reputation of a fabulously prolific artist. One of the most important of such works consisted in three altarpieces and thirty-nine ceiling paintings for the Jesuit church (now St. Charles Borromeo) at Antwerp. The contract for these, signed at the beginning of 1620, stipulated that they must be ready by the beginning of 1621 and that Rubens must paint the sketches himself, though his assistants might help with the final execution. The ceiling paintings, set in wooden coffers, were all destroyed by fire in 1718. The oil sketches, many of which have survived, show not only how skilfully Rubens managed – the first time this was done in Northern Europe – to represent the ceiling scenes *di sotto in su* in the Venetian manner, but also how he imparted an ethereal lightness to his figures, which give the impression of being suffused by light. This was not only a consequence of the subject-matter but also of Rubens's developed artistic insight: the local colouring was gradually subdued and the tone at the same time enriched, while the firm contours dissolved in an increasingly picturesque composition. Apart from the church decoration Rubens executed other important commissions for the Jesuits, who, as a learned Order, took great interest in the intellectual and artistic traditions of antiquity and of the Christian centuries; they also patronized the arts as a means of spreading the faith and encouraging the laity to take a livelier interest in religion. Rubens's talent, ripened in the Italian sun, his energy, versatility and devotion to Catholicism, made him their favourite contemporary artist.

Probably at the beginning of 1622, Louis XIII of France ordered from Rubens the designs for a series of twelve tapestries on *The History of the Emperor Constantine*. The Emperor's respect for his mother Helena plays an important part in the story, which was recommended to the King by counsellors aware of the jealous relations between him and his mother, Marie de' Medici. At about the same time, in 1622-25, Rubens painted for the Queen Mother a series of twenty-five pictures representing the events of her life in metaphorical and allegorical style, and intended as decoration for one of the galleries in the Palais du Luxembourg in Paris. This commission brought Rubens into contact with one of the richest and most splendid courts of Europe. The series, now in the Louvre, is one of his most elaborate undertakings and an outstanding monument of Baroque art. As he wrote in 1621: "Each one according to his gifts: my endowments are such that I have never lacked courage to undertake any design, however vast in size or diversified in subject."

Another commission, this time from the Infanta Isabella, daughter of Philip II of Spain, gave him a fresh opportunity to indulge his preference for grandiose compositions. Isabella, now in middle age, wished to make a royal donation as a sign of her attachment to the convent of Poor Clares in Madrid, where she had lived as a girl and received part of her education. As she had in her retinue the greatest artistic genius of the age, and as her court was at Brussels, the principal tapestry centre of the world, she naturally fell on the idea of presenting the convent with a set of tapestries designed by Rubens. Thus originated the series known as *The Triumph of the Eucharist*, woven at Brussels by Jan Raes, Jacob Geubels and their assistants. The cartoons for these twenty tapestries were preceded by various sketches, made in 1625-27.

Even if Rubens had never held a paintbrush, he would be known to posterity on account of his diplomatic career. As an agent and adviser of the Regent Isabella he devoted himself to the task of inducing the Dutch insurgents to return to the Catholic church and submit once more to the Spanish monarchy. The first evidence of his diplomatic activity is a letter in his hand dating from 1623, which, however, indicates that he was engaged in secret state affairs at an earlier date. He believed sincerely and profoundly in the possibility of making peace between the Southern and Northern Netherlands and thus reviving the prosperity of his sorely tried country. At first he was confident that direct negotiations would succeed, but gradually he came to believe that the only hope lay in a treaty between Spain and England, as the latter country was supporting the Dutch. From 1627 onwards he devoted all his powers to this end, and in 1629-30 he visited Madrid and London. Although his good offices were valued by both sides, his efforts were in vain. At his last audience with Charles I of England he was made a knight and loaded with presents; he then returned home and withdrew from political life, though later his services were used sporadically in negotiations between the Southern and Northern Netherlands.

His extra-artistic activity was not without influence on his art, which he used to some extent as a counter in the political game. For instance, he presented the King of England with a picture illustrating *The Blessings of Peace*, to induce him to reach agreement wit Spain. In Madrid he was able to renew acquaintance with Titian's work, which he had so much admired and copied many years earlier, and again he copied many of the great Venetian's paintings with reverent devotion. Titian's later work, in which the force of light resolves the local colour into

Château de Steen (Detail), National Gallery, London

The Three Graces, Museo del Prado, Madrid

Hélène Fourment and Two of Her Children, Musée du Louvre, Paris

Madonna with Saints, St. Jacobs-church, Antwerp

a sparkling multiplicity of separate elements, inspired Rubens to continue in the direction he had already chosen. From this time on his touch became freer and more rhythmical, his forms lighter, more fluent and animated.

In 1626, after seventeen years of marriage, Rubens's wife Isabella died. Their only daughter, Clara Serena, had died three years earlier at the age of twelve, and Rubens's happy home life now lay in ruins. No doubt he was partially distracted by the busy diplomatic life and foreign travel of 1628-30, and on returning to Antwerp he threw himself into painting with renewed vigour; but he was depressed by loneliness and felt the need to remarry. In 1630, at the age of fifty-three, he took as his bride the sixteen-year-old Helena, a girl of great beauty and the youngest daughter of his old friend and neighbour Daniel Fourment. Helena not only made Rubens happy in his last years but also served repeatedly as a source of artistic inspiration.

In the thirties Rubens's personality developed to its fullest exuberance. This is the period of some of his finest altarpieces, such as *The San Ildefonso*, commissioned by the Archduchess Isabella for Saint-Jacques-sur-Coudenberg in Brussels, and *The Madonna with Saints*, painted to adorn Rubens's own memorial chapel. In addition he continued to paint large cyclical and decorative works. At a somewhat earlier date he had painted several *Hunting Scenes* which served as the basis for a series of tapestries, and in the first half of the thirties he designed cartoons for *The History of Achilles*. No documents on the origin of this series of eight pieces have survived, but it was probably ordered for a particular customer by Rubens's father-in-law Daniel Fourment, who was a well-to-do tapestry dealer.

Some years before, it was indicated to Rubens that the English court intended to call on his services for the decoration of the ceiling of the king's magnificent Banqueting House in Whitehall, London, built by Inigo Jones and almost completed by 1622. He did not actually receive the commission, however, until 1629, during his stay in London. At the wish of Charles I, the nine compartments of the large ceiling were to be filled with scenes illustrating the blessings of the reign of his father James I. Rubens went to work on the designs immediately after his return to Antwerp, but owing to various circumstances the nine paintings were not placed in position until 1635.

Having delivered the last pictures for the *Medici Gallery* in the Palais du Luxembourg in 1625, Rubens had hoped to begin at once on the gallery which formed a counterpart to it and was to be decorated with scenes from the life of Marie de' Medici's consort Henry IV. Although the commission failed to materialize he continued to work on the project, even after his return from London in 1630. However, it did not get beyond a few oil sketches and unfinished canvases: the powerful Cardinal Richelieu, knowing Rubens's Spanish sympathies and anxious to prevent a treaty between France and Spain, opposed the plan to such purpose that it was abandoned.

In the last years of his life Rubens received two more commissions of special importance. His great patroness the Archduchess Isabella died in 1633, and Philip IV of Spain appointed his brother, the Cardinal Infante Ferdinand, to succeed her as governor of the Southern Netherlands. The Infante's arrival was delayed by warlike operations in Germany, but on 17 April 1635 he finally made his Joyous Entry into Antwerp. The city's trade had suffered badly from the political situation, and the magistrates planned a festive reception on a large scale in order to win favour with the new governor. Rubens, who was a decorator first and foremost, thus had the unique opportunity of decorating a whole city. He was put in general charge of the work and provided with numerous assistants. Triumphal arches and 'stages', adorned with painting and sculpture, were set up along the route that the governor and his suite were to follow. In the grandiose arches and porticoes Rubens displayed his talent as an architect, while the decoration bore witness to his knowledge of mythology and sense of allegory. Three years later, in 1638, he was again commissioned by the Antwerp municipality to design decorations in honour of the Cardinal Infante: the latter had won a victory over the Dutch at Kallo, and shortly afterwards the Spanish troops at St. Omer defeated the French, who were allied with Holland. To commemorate these successes and in the continued hope of securing the governor's favour, the city fathers planned to attach a special victory car to the customary procession held annually as a municipal festival. The car was designed in accordance with an oil sketch by Rubens.

Rubens received his last major commission from Philip IV of Spain, a great admirer of his work, who ordered a set of pictures – mostly

mythological subjects from Ovid's *Metamorphoses*, but including some
hunting scenes and animal pieces – to decorate the Torre de la Parada,
a new royal hunting lodge near Madrid. In 1636 Rubens had been
appointed court painter to the Infante Ferdinand, the post he had occupied at the court of Albert and Isabella since his return from Italy
in 1608. The commission for the Torre de la Parada is first mentioned
in a letter of that year from Ferdinand to his royal brother, stating
that Rubens had received it and had begun on some of the paintings.
Their exact number is not mentioned in the letter or in later
documents, but these give some idea of the huge scale of the undertaking, which must have comprised about a hundred and fifteen pictures.
Rubens himself designed the mythological pieces and the task must
have taken his mind back to Giulio Romano's murals depicting classical
legends in the Palazzo del Tè, which he admired so much in his youth.
A few of the large final versions are also in Rubens's own hand, but
most of them were done by colleagues of established reputation. The
animal pieces were mostly painted by Paul de Vos, a specialist in this
line, while Pieter Snayers painted some landscapes with a staffage of
hunting scenes. The whole series was despatched to Madrid by the
beginning of 1638. About forty of the final versions of paintings
designed by Rubens have survived, and about fifty oil sketches. These
small panels are real gems of their kind and are among the finest examples of Rubens's vision and style in his latest period: golden in tone
and loosely executed in a free, flowing style, they testify to the strength
and unimpaired liveliness of his imagination.

After Rubens's important diplomatic journeys were over his life
became quieter, but no less productive. Always in good health apart
from occasional attacks of gout, he lived out his days in the company
of his beloved Helena, who presented him with five children. What
conjugal life meant to him is abudantly expressed in his symbolic painting *The Garden of Love*. As far as possible he spent his time at the
Château de Steen, the country house which he bought in 1635 at Elewijt
near Vilvoorde. He took long walks and rides through the woods
and meadows, which he then painted with love. In these spacious and
lyrical landscapes, marvels of light and colour, he projected his own
vision, half-way between reality and imagination, and depicted luxuriant nature as an expression of the inexhaustible vigour and fertility

of the earth. In his many explorations of the countryside he became familiar, as if for the first time, with the life of the local peasants, bound to the soil. He saw with sympathy how they toiled in the fields and returned to the farmstead at sunset, exhausted but content with their labours. All this he put in his pictures as the great Pieter Bruegel had done before him. He also noted the fairs and country festivals in which the rustics gave vent to their Dionysiac passions. However, the paintings in which he recorded their animal orgies and carouses, and in which the ground seems to vibrate under the impact of the round dance, are largely the work of his imagination, which saw the peasants, like plants and animals, as part of the luxuriance and vital force of nature.

During his last years, with the youthful Helena Fourment by his side, Rubens was able to keep old age at bay, but the fire of his temperament was dimmed at times by a touching softness. The colouring of his pictures often appeared as an iridescent glow, expressing the marvellous gradations of blossoming and fading and the melancholy of one who feels that the inexorable transience of the world will soon put an end to his happiness.

At the beginning of 1640 Rubens's health began to fail. His attacks of gout grew more frequent and rapidly undermined his strength; on 30 May his heart succumbed and he died in his house in Antwerp.

Rubens dominated the artistic life of his time by his versatility and power of execution. There is no other instance in the history of art of such absolute authority and undisputed triumph. His works were so revered as to exercise a universal influence. Throughout his life, in whatever innovation he undertook he was imitated by admiring colleagues. The ablest of these understood his purpose and were inspired by the deeper meaning of his robust, impetuous art; weaker personalities, discerning only superficial features, imitated these and often sank into a dull, anaemic style. His influence on later generations was no less powerful: his art was the reflection of his own personality rather than of his time, and it continued to hold sway accordingly. In the three centuries since his death he has sometimes been extravagantly praised and sometimes much over-criticized, but never forgotten. Watteau in the early eighteenth century admired Rubens's work, copying many of his drawings and making a thorough study of the Medici cycle. At the end of that century Sir Joshua Reynolds drew attention to his amazing expertise, while some years later Constable lectured on his landscapes. No one, however, took such a passionate interest in Rubens as Delacroix, who admired his treatment of the visible world and power to evoke both drama and tenderer feelings, and who perceived the importance of colour in achieving these effects. Renoir, one of the few painters who could compare with Rubens as far as the female nude was concerned, studied his technique and envied the ease with which he imparted warmth and life to the flesh with a few light touches. Even Cézanne looked up to him and was often inspired by his example. To all these artists Rubens's historical background was of little or no significance: no special exposition was needed, the princely splendour of his art sufficed to command their allegiance.

R.-A. D'HULST

ABBREVIATIONS

Alpers: S. Alpers, *The Decoration of the Torre de la Parada, Corpus Rubenianum Ludwig Burchard*, IX, Brussels, 1971.

Baudouin: F. Baudouin, *Rubens en zijn eeuw*, Antwerp, 1972.

Bock-Rosenberg: E. Bock and J. Rosenberg, *Staatliche Museen zu Berlin. Die Zeichnungen alter Meister im Kupferstichkabinett. Die niederländischen Meister*, I-II, Berlin, 1930.

Brussels, 1965: Cat. Exh. *De eeuw van Rubens*, Koninklijke Musea voor Schone Kunsten van België, Brussels, 1965.

Burchard: L. Burchard, *Catalogue of a Loan Exhibition of Works by Peter Paul Rubens, Kt*, Wildenstein, London, 1950.

Burchard-d'Hulst, 1956: L. Burchard and R.-A. d'Hulst, Cat. Exh. *Tekeningen van P.P. Rubens*, Rubenshouse, Antwerp, 1956.

Burchard-d'Hulst, 1963: L. Burchard and R.-A. d'Hulst, *Rubens Drawings*, I-II, Brussels, 1963.

d'Hulst, 1968: R.-A. d'Hulst, *Olieverfschetsen van Rubens uit Nederlands en Belgisch openbaar bezit*, s.l., 1968.

Evers, 1942: H.G. Evers, *Peter Paul Rubens*, Munich, 1942.

Evers, 1943: H.G. Evers, *Rubens und sein Werk, neue Forschungen*, Brussels, 1943.

Glück: G. Glück, *Rubens, Van Dyck und ihr Kreis*, Vienna, 1943.

Glück-Haberditzl: G. Glück and F.M. Haberditzl, *Die Handzeichnungen von Peter Paul Rubens*, Berlin, 1928.

Goris-Held: J.-A. Goris and J.S. Held, *Rubens in America*, Antwerp, 1947.

Haverkamp Begemann: E. Haverkamp Begemann, *The Achilles Series, Corpus Rubenianum Ludwig Burchard*, X, Brussels, 1975.

Held: J.S. Held, *Rubens, Selected Drawings*, I-II, London, 1959.

Huemer, Portraits I: Frances Huemer, *Portraits I, Corpus Rubenianum Ludwig Burchard*, XIX, Brussels, 1977.

K.d.K.: P.P. Rubens, des Meisters Gemälde, ed. R. Oldenbourg, Klassiker der Kunst, V, Stuttgart-Berlin, 1921.

K.d.K., ed. Rosenberg: P.P. Rubens, Des Meisters Gemälde, ed. A. Rosenberg, Klassiker der Kunst, V, Stuttgart-Leipzig, 1906.

Lugt, Louvre, Ecole flamande, II, 1949: F. Lugt, *Musée du Louvre, Inventaire général des dessins des écoles du Nord. Ecole flamande*, II, Paris, 1949.

Martin, Ceiling Paintings: J.R. Martin, *The Ceiling Paintings for the Jesuit Church in Antwerp, Corpus Rubenianum Ludwig Burchard*, I, Brussels, 1968.

Martin, Pompa Introitus: J.R. Martin, *The Decorations for the Pompa Introitus Ferdinandi, Corpus Rubenianum Ludwig Burchard*, XVI, Brussels, 1972.

Oldenbourg: R. Oldenbourg, *Peter Paul Rubens, ed. W. von Bode*, Berlin, 1922.

Reiset: F. Reiset, *Notice des Dessins, etc. au Musée National du Louvre*, I, Paris, 1866.

Rooses: M. Rooses, *L'œuvre de P.P. Rubens, histoire et description de ses tableaux et dessins*, I-V, Antwerp, 1886-92.

Rooses-Ruelens: Correspondance de Rubens et documents épistolaires concernant sa vie et ses œuvres, publiés, traduits, annotés par Ch. Ruelens (I), par M. Rooses et feu Ch. Ruelens (II-VI), Antwerp, 1887-1909.

Rotterdam, 1953-54: Cat. Exh. *Olieverfschetsen van Rubens*, Museum Boymans, Rotterdam, 1953-54.

Rubens-Bulletijn: Rubens-Bulletijn, Jaarboeken der ambtelijke Commissie ingesteld door den Gemeenteraad der Stad Antwerpen voor het uitgeven van Bescheiden betrekkelijk het Leven en de Werken van Rubens, I-V, Antwerp, 1882-1910.

Schönbrunner-Meder: J. Schönbrunner en J. Meder, *Handzeichnungen alter Meister aus der Albertina und anderen Sammlungen*, Vienna, 1896-1908.

Smith, Catalogue Raisonné: J. Smith, *A Catalogue Raisonné of the Works of the most Eminent Dutch, Flemish and French Painters*, I-IX, London, 1829-1942.

Thuillier-Foucart: J. Thuillier and J. Foucart, *Le storie di Maria de' Medici, di Rubens al Lussemburgo*, Milan, 1967.

Van Puyvelde: L. Van Puyvelde, *Rubens*, Paris-Brussels, 1952.

Van Puyvelde, Esquisses: L. Van Puyvelde, *Les Esquisses de Rubens*, Basel, 1948.

Vlieghe, Saints: H. Vlieghe, *Saints*, I-II, *Corpus Rubenianum Ludwig Burchard*, VIII, Brussels, 1973.

CATALOGUE
Paintings and Oilsketches

A variation on the classical theme of 'Hercules at the crossroads', symbolizing the conflict between man's higher and lower nature. A youth, beset by the temptations of Bacchus and Venus, has sunk to the ground and is on the point of yielding; but Minerva and Chronos, guardians of wisdom, appear in the nick of time, and their victory is presaged by the genii who are seen on the right.

The subject derives from an engraving by Pieter Perret executed before 1585, to a design by Rubens's teacher Otto van Veen. Although it bears Van Veen's monogram, the style of the painting is more plastic than is usual with him, and we may suppose that the young Rubens had at least some part in it. The picture may have been signed and sold by Van Veen because Rubens was much less well known and, being an apprentice, was not entitled to sell works of art himself. The painting is an important document from the point of view of the relationship between Rubens's work and that of his master.

Panel, 146 : 212 cm; monogrammed *OV*.

Bibl.: F.M. Haberditzl, *Die Lehrer des Rubens*, in *Jahrbuch der kunsthistorischen Sammlungen des allerhöchsten Kaiserhauses*, XXVII, 1908, pp. 209-13; J. Müller Hofstede, *Zur Antwerpener Frühzeit von Peter Paul Rubens*, in *Münchener Jahrbuch der bildenden Künste*, 1962, pp. 179-215.

Prov.: Owned by Queen Christina of Sweden.

Nationalmuseum, Stockholm

Paul, at that time still named Saul and a persecutor of the Christians, was on his way to Damascus when he was thrown violently to the ground and heard a voice saying: "Saul, Saul, why persecutest thou me?" (*Acts*, 9 : 1-9; 22 : 6-10; 26 : 12-20).

In accordance with tradition Saul is shown on horseback, while Christ appears in a dazzling light in the clouds. This early work is inspired by an engraving (1545) by Eneo Vico after Francesco Salviati and by Leonardo da Vinci's *Battle of Anghiari*; other details, including the figure of Christ, are still reminiscent of Rubens's master Otto van Veen. It was J. Müller Hofstede who, in 1964, first assigned the work to Rubens and to his Italian period, *c.* 1602.

Panel, 72 : 103 cm.

Bibl.:   J. Müller Hofstede, *An Early Rubens Conversion of St. Paul. The Beginning of his Preoccupation with Leonardo's Battle of Anghiari*, in *The Burlington Magazine*, CVI, 1964, pp. 95-106.

Prov.:   Roose family, Antwerp.

Private collection, Courtrai (Kortrijk)

The well-known legend of the young Roman officer and martyr, popularized by Jacopo de Voragine (*Legenda Aurea*, I, cols. 170-1), is derived from the *Acta* of Sebastian, erroneously ascribed to St. Ambrose. He is stated there to have been a centurion whom the Emperor Diocletian in 287 condemned to be shot by archers; as he did not succumb to his wounds, he was finally clubbed to death.

The martyr is here seen transfixed by arrows; according to legend he was freed and tended by a widow named Irene, but in the painting he is succoured by four angels. On the left is Sebastian's breastplate, a motif probably of Italian origin: it occurs in the same position and similarly emphasized in Titian's *St. Sebastian* in the Hermitage at Leningrad.

The painting undoubtedly belongs to Rubens's Italian period; the style may be compared with that of *The Baptism of Christ*, a drawing of *c.* 1604 now in the Louvre in Paris (see No. 121).

Canvas, 153 : 118 cm.

Bibl.:   F.M. Haberditzl, *Studien über Rubens*, in *Jahrbuch der kusthistorischen Sammlungen des allerhöchsten Kaiserhauses*, XXX, 1912, p. 259; *Glück*, pp. 375, 409; *Evers, 1942*, p. 143; *Evers, 1943*, pp. 151, 202; C. Norris, Review of L. van Puyvelde, *La peinture flamande à Rome*, in *The Burlington Magazine*, XCV, 1953, p. 108; *Held*, p. 98; *Burchard-d'Hulst, 1963*, pp. 54, 110; *Vlieghe, Saints*, II, pp. 147, 148, No. 144.

Prov.:   Cardinal Neri Corsini (1685-1770); acquired by the Italian Government from Prince Tommaso Corsini, 1884.

Galleria Nazionale d'Arte Antica, Palazzo Corsini, Rome

Leander swam nightly across the Hellespont from Abydos to Sestos to see his beloved Hero. She lit a lamp to guide him, but one night it blew out, he failed to reach Sestos and was drowned. Hero in despair threw herself into the sea. (Ovid, *Heroides*, 18, 19).

The naked, swollen body of the dead Leander occupies the centre of the composition. He is surrounded by thirteen Nereids, swimming in a stormy sea.

This work was ascribed to Rubens in 1958 by M. Jaffé, who assigned it to his Italian period. The date 1604-05 is generally accepted. Several sheets of study drawings, especially for the Nereids, have survived.

Canvas, 95,9 : 127 cm.

Bibl.:   M. Jaffé, *Rubens in Italy: Rediscovered Works*, in *The Burlington Magazine*, C, 1958, pp. 418-21; J. Müller Hofstede, *Some Early Drawings by Rubens*, in *Master Drawings*, II, 1964, pp. 8-10; M. Jaffé, *A Sheet of Drawings from Rubens's Italian Period*, in *Master Drawings*, VIII, 1970, pp. 42-51.

Prov.: Mrs. Carlsson; Mrs. Frederick W. Hilles.

Yale University Art Gallery, Gift of Susan Morse Hilles, New Haven, Connecticut

Although this painting is generally called *The Entombment*, it is in fact a *Lamentation* (the scene after the *Descent from the Cross* and before the *Entombment*). The body of Christ is surrounded by the Virgin, bending over his face, Mary Magdalen clasping his ankles, Joseph of Arimathea, Nicodemus, St. John and some lamenting women.

The picture bears on its back the seal of the noble Roman family of Colonna, and it is listed in the inventory, dated 1783, of art treasures in the Colonna palace outside Rome. In 1605-6, when Rubens was in Italy, his brother Philip was secretary and librarian to Cardinal Ascanio Colonna (1559-1608), and it may be supposed that the picture was painted then and was commissioned by the Cardinal. A larger work for which it might have served as model is not known to exist.

Copper, 28,2 : 24,4 cm.

Bibl.:   Cat. Exh. *Rotterdam, 1953-54*, pp. 32, 33, No. 2.

Prov.:   Cardinal Ascanio Colonna (1559-1608)?; Palazzo Colonna, Rome, 1783; presented in 1798 by Prince Philippo Colonna, Duke of Paliano, to the painter Giuseppe Cades (1750-99); Harry G. Sperling, New York.

Cummer Gallery of Art, Jacksonville, Florida

A portrait of Gian-Carlo Doria, Duke of Tursis, born at Genoa in 1577, son of the Doge Agostino Doria. His brother, Giacomo Massimiliano, was the husband of Brigida Spinola Doria, whose portrait Rubens also painted (see No. 7). Gian-Carlo was a naval commander in the service of Philip III of Spain, and his breastplate accordingly bears the cross of the Order of St. James of Compostela. Some elements of the painting are symbolic, e.g. the eagle's nest in the tree, which figures in the arms of the Doria family. The portrait was certainly painted in Rubens's Italian period.

Canvas, 265 : 188 cm.

Bibl.: R. Longhi, *Un ritratto equestre dell' epoca genovese del Rubens*, in *Annuaire des Musées Royaux des Beaux-Arts de Belgique*, II, 1939, pp. 123-30; J. Müller Hofstede, *Rubens' St. Georg und seine frühen Reiterbildnisse*, in *Zeitschrift für Kunstgeschichte*, XXVIII, 1965, pp. 84-90; *Huemer, Portraits I*, No. 10.

Prov.: Doria family, Genoa; inherited by the Doria d'Angri branch in Naples in the first half of the nineteenth century; Doria d'Angri sale, Naples, 27 February 1940, lot 172; sold to Hitler by Mussolini's order; traced in Germany and restored to Italy, 1948; Ufficio Recupero, Rome; on loan to the Palazzo Vecchio, Florence.

Soprintendenza per i Beni Artistici e Storici per le Provincie di Firenze e Pistoia, Florence

Horsin Déon noted in 1851 that this portrait was formerly inscribed on the back: *Brigida Spinola Doria, Anni Sal. 1606, Aet. Suae 22, P.P. Rubens Ft.* The same inscription, except for the artist's name, figures on a lithograph made after the painting in 1848 by Pierre-Frédéric Lehnert: this shows the Marchesa (born at Genoa in 1584) full-length, on a terrace with a garden visible to the left. It appears therefore that the portrait was originally larger and that a third of it was cut off at the bottom, as well as narrow strips on both sides. It was painted at Genoa *c.* 1606. Rubens also made other portraits of the Marchesa, which all show her in a chair.

The portraits painted by Rubens at Genoa, such as this one, established the model which Van Dyck imitated when he came to work there fifteen years later.

Canvas, 152,2:98,7 cm.

Bibl.:   Horsin Déon, *De la conservation et de la restauration des tableaux*, Paris, 1851, pp. 34, 35; *Rooses*, IV, p. 273, No. 1064; K. Bauch, *Beiträge zur Rubensforschung*, in *Jahrbuch der preussischen Kunstsammlungen*, XXXXV, 1924, p. 190; L. Burchard, *Genuesische Frauenbildnisse von Rubens*, in *Jahrbuch der preussischen Kunstsammlungen*, L, 1929, pp. 321-3; *Goris-Held*, p. 26, No. 2; M. Jaffé, *Some Recent Acquisitions of Seventeenth-Century Flemish Painting*, in *National Gallery of Art, Report and Studies in the History of Art*, 1969, pp. 26, 29, 33, n. 59; *Huemer, Portraits I*, No. 41.

Prov.:   Bertram Currie, Minley Manor, Hampshire; Duveen Brothers Inc., New York; Samuel H. Kress Collection, 1961.

National Gallery of Art, Samuel H. Kress Collection, 1961, Washington

Susanna, a Jewess living at Babylon, was accused of adultery by two elders of Israel who had tried in vain to seduce her; she was condemned to death, but was saved at the last minute by the sagacity of Daniel, the future prophet (*Daniel*, 13:1-65).

The painting shows the naked Susanna surprised in her bath by the two elders. Rubens depicted this scene many times, and several versions are preserved. The present, as far as is known, is the earliest; it was painted during his years in Italy. See No. 33.

Canvas, 94:66 cm.

Bibl.: *K.d.K.*, p. 19; A. De Rinaldis, *La Galleria Borghese in Roma*, Rome, 1939, p. 41; Paola della Pergola, *Galleria Borghese. I Dipinti*, II, Rome, 1959, pp. 183, 184, No. 273; Paola della Pergola, *P.P. Rubens e il tema della Susanna al bagno*, in *Bulletin van de Koninklijke Musea voor Schone Kunsten van België*, 1967, pp. 7-22.

Prov.: In the Villa Borghese from the first half of the seventeenth century.

Museo e Galleria Borghese, Rome

This group portrait raises several perplexing questions as to the date of execution and the identity of the figures. The only certain facts are that the man facing the spectator is Rubens himself; Mantuan motifs are visible in the background landscape; and the work was painted during Rubens's stay in Italy.

Canvas, 77,5 : 101 cm.

Bibl.: K. Gerstenberg, *Rubens im Kreise seiner römischen Gefährten*, in *Zeitschrift für Kunstgeschichte*, I, 1932, pp. 99-109; *Glück*, pp. 392, 393; *Evers, 1942*, pp. 27, 459, 463; *Evers, 1943*, pp. 321-6; H. Kaufmann, *Peter Paul Rubens im Licht seiner Selbstbekenntnisse*, in *Wallraf-Richartz-Jahrbuch*, XVII, 1955, p. 181; W.J. Müller, *Das Selbstbildnis des Rubens mit seinen Mantuaner Freunden*, in *Kunstgeschichtliche Gesellschaft zu Berlin. Sitzungsberichte*, N.F., Heft 11, October 1962-May 1963, pp. 5-7; H. Vey-Annamaria Kesting, *Katalog der niederländischen Gemälde von 1550 bis 1800 im Wallraf-Richartz-Museum und im öffentlichen Besitz der Stadt Köln*, Cologne, 1967, pp. 94, 95, No. Dep. 248; I. Bini, *Un Rubens del periodo Mantovano a Colonia*, in *Civiltà Mantovana*, VIII, 1974, pp. 293-303; *Huemer, Portraits I*, No. 37.

Prov.: Lord Byron, Newstead Abbey, sold March 1722?; G.T. Biddulph, Petersham; Dr. Vitale Bloch, Berlin; Eugen Abresch, Neustadt an der Haardt; loaned by the Federal Republic of Germany.

Wallraf-Richartz-Museum, Cologne

The Gonzaga family adoring the Trinity, Museo del Palazzo Ducale, Mantua

While at Mantua Rubens painted for Duke Vinzenzo I Gonzaga three large pictures for the Cappella Maggiore in the former Jesuit church of the Santissima Trinità: *The Gonzaga family adoring the Trinity*, which was to be placed over the altar, and, for the side-walls of the choir, *The Transfiguration* (now at Nancy) and *The Baptism of Christ* (now at Antwerp). These paintings, begun in August 1604 at earliest, were completed in May 1605. The central one depicted the reigning Duke Vincenzo Gonzaga and his wife Eleonora de' Medici, with the Duke's deceased parents Ferdinando I and Eleanor of Austria. Behind these four central figures were the five children of the marriage and three bodyguards, two on the left and one on the right.

In 1797 a French 'commissaire de guerre' had the centre painting cut to pieces, and portions of it were dispersed. However, in 1797-1800 the restorer Felice Campi pieced together some of the main sections to form a canvas that is now in the Palazzo Ducale at Mantua. This shows Vincenzo and his father kneeling in worship on the left, and Eleonora and her mother-in-law on the right. Some portraits of the ducal children are still dispersed in various collections (see Nos. 10, 11), while other details from the painting (see No. 12) are preserved separately in the Palazzo Ducale.

This portrait, published by C. Norris, is a fragment of *The Gonzaga family adoring the Trinity*, formerly in the church of the Santissima Trinità at Mantua, which showed the sons of Duke Vincenzo I kneeling on the left beside their father (see p. 41). Ferdinando, aged seventeen, wears a black, white-collared doublet embroidered with a Maltese cross. His head is seen against the background of a halberdier's red cloak with gold ornamentation. A leg clad in armour can also be seen behind him, showing that the boy was in a kneeling posture.

Canvas, 48 : 38,2 cm.

Bibl.: Ch. Norris, *The Tempio della Santissima Trinità at Mantua*, in *The Burlington Magazine*, CXVII, 1975, pp. 73-9.

Prov.: Private collection, England.

Private collection, Wassenaar, Netherlands

A fragment of *The Gonzaga family adoring the Trinity*, formerly in the church of the Santissima Trinità at Mantua, which showed the sons of Duke Vincenzo I kneeling on the left beside their father (see p. 41). There is disagreement as to which son is here portrayed. Traditionally it is supposed to be Francesco, but C. Norris believes it to be the young Vincenzo. In the right background can be seen the arm and Maltese cross of Ferdinando, another son of the Duke (see No. 10).

Canvas, 67:51,5 cm.

Bibl.: M. Jaffé, *The Deceased Young Duke of Mantua's Brother*, in *The Burlington Magazine*, CIII, 1961, pp. 374-8; C. Norris, *The Tempio della Santissima Trinità at Mantua*, in *The Burlington Magazine*, CXVII, 1975, pp. 73-9.

Prov.: In the possession of the Vienna museum since 1908.

Kunsthistorisches Museum, Vienna

Fragment of *The Gonzaga family adoring the Trinity*, formerly in the church of the Santissima Trinità at Mantua (see p. 41). This figure, of which only the head and the left arm remain, was most probably on the extreme left of the original composition. In the background is a fragment of a Salomonic column, a frequent motif in Rubens's work. Columns of this shape, believed to come from the Temple in Jerusalem, were in old St. Peter's in Rome and were much admired by the archaeologists of Rubens's time. See No. 122.

Canvas, 128:69 cm.

Bibl.: M. Jaffé, *The Deceased Young Duke of Mantua's Brother*, in *The Burlington Magazine*, CIII, 1961, pp. 374-8; Frances Huemer, *Some Observations on Rubens' Mantua Altarpiece*, in *The Art Bulletin*, XLVIII, 1966, pp. 84, 85; J.S. Held, *Letter to the Editor*, in *The Art Bulletin*, XLVIII, 1966, pp. 468-9; C. Norris, *The Tempio della Santissima Trinità at Mantua*, in *The Burlington Magazine*, CXVII, 1975, pp. 73-9.

Prov.: Church of the Santissima Trinità, Mantua.

Museo del Palazzo Ducale, Mantua

This portrait is to be compared with one in Vienna (see No. 11) which formed part of *The Gonzaga family adoring the Trinity*: in that painting, formerly in the church of the Santissima Trinità at Mantua, Duke Vincenzo and his sons were depicted kneeling together (see p. 41). M. Jaffé, who first published the portrait and ascribed it to Rubens, believes it to be of Francesco, the eldest son, who succeeded his father as fifth Duke of Mantua.

Canvas, 67,3 : 57,2 cm.

Bibl.: *Rooses*, IV, p. 209, No. 985; M. Jaffé, *The Deceased Young Duke of Mantua's Brother*, in *The Burlington Magazine*, CIII, 1961, pp. 374-8; C. Norris, *The Tempio della Santissima Trinità at Mantua*, in *The Burlington Magazine*, CXVII, 1975, pp. 73-9; *Huemer, Portraits I*, No. 15.

Prov.: King Charles I of England; purchased by Mr. Bass in 1649; first recorded in the Saltram collection in 1819.

The National Trust (Saltram), Plympton

The Virgin, seated left of centre, averts her gaze from the pain inflicted on her son. Beside her are two women looking up to heaven, as angels hover round a dazzling light that breaks through the clouds. On the right is the priest performing the operation, with two assistants; Simeon stands behind. On the far left are three women onlookers, one with a child.

A careful modello, executed *c.* 1607, for the altarpiece still in the Jesuit church of Sant' Ambrogio at Genoa, which was commissioned by the Marchese Niccolò Pallavicini, banker to the Duke of Mantua.

Canvas transferred to panel, 105 : 74 cm.

Bibl.:   *Rooses*, I, pp. 201-3, under No. 156; R. Eigenberger, *Die Gemäldegalerie der Akademie der bildenden Künste in Wien*, Vienna-Leipzig, 1927, pp. 346, 347; J. Müller Hofstede, *Bildnisse aus Rubens' Italienjahre*, in *Jahrbuch der Staatlichen Kunstsammlungen in Baden-Württenberg*, II, 1965, pp. 89-154.

Prov.:   Very probably identical with the work of the same title recorded in Rubens's estate at his death; appears in David Teniers's painting of *Archduke Leopold William visiting his gallery*, now in the Prado at Madrid; Count Anton Lamberg-Sprinzenstein, Vienna, who bequeathed it to the Academy in 1821.

Gemäldegalerie der Akademie der bildenden Künste, Vienna

In 1607, during his stay in Italy, Rubens received an important commission from the clergy of the Oratorian Chiesa Nuova in Rome, also called Santa Maria in Vallicella. The church possessed a miraculous Madonna that was only exhibited on great feast-days. Rubens was to paint a picture for the high altar showing this Madonna being worshipped by the patron saints of the church. When the panel was completed and installed, however, it proved to be too shiny, and he decided to replace it by three separate paintings on slate. Having tried unsuccessfully to sell the panel to the Duke of Mantua, he took it back with him to Antwerp in 1608 and had it placed over the tomb of his mother, who died in that year, in St. Michael's Abbey (which no longer exists). The panel is now in the Grenoble museum. According to L. Burchard the present sketch is connected with this altarpiece, though it is not clear where it figures in the process of evolution. St. Gregory, wearing the papal *zucchetto*, is depicted in the centre; on the left are St. Mark, seen from behind, and St. Papianus, while St. Domitilla is in profile on the right. The figure of St. Mark is borrowed from Correggio's *Madonna with St. George*, which Rubens had had an oppurtunity of admiring at Modena near Mantua. See No. 16.

Canvas, 146,5 : 120 cm.

Bibl.: L. Burchard, *Skizzen des jungen Rubens*, in *Sitzungsberichte der kunstgeschichtlichen Gesellschaft Berlin*, October 1926-May 1927, p. 2, No. 3; *Evers, 1943*, pp. 111-4; Cat. Exh. *Rotterdam, 1953-54*, p. 54; *Vlieghe, Saints*, II, pp. 54, 55, No. 109d.

Prov.: King Frederick II of Prussia; Schloss Charlottenburg, Berlin; Neues Schloss, Potsdam. On permanent loan in the Berlin museum since 1966.

Staatliche Museen Preussischer Kulturbesitz, Gemäldegalerie, Berlin-West

In 1607 Rubens painted a *St. Gregory the Great with other saints* for the high altar of the Chiesa Nuova in Rome, also called Santa Maria in Vallicella. When installed, however, the painting did not meet with approval as it was too shiny, so he undertook to replace it (see No. 15). This he did with three separate paintings: one for the high altar itself, showing the Madonna worshipped by angels, and two pictures of three saints apiece to decorate the walls of the apse on either side of the altar. All three were painted on slate to minimize the reflection of light. The work seen here is an oil sketch for the main painting, which was completed in 1608 and is still in place over the high altar. See No. 123.

Canvas, 86 : 57 cm.

Bibl.:   *K.d.K.*, p. 24; R. Eigenberger, *Die Gemäldegalerie der Akademie der bildenden Künste in Wien*, Vienna-Leipzig, 1927, pp. 334-6; *Evers, 1943*, p. 117; *Held*, pp. 100, 101, No. 17.

Prov.:   Count Anton Lamberg-Sprinzenstein, Vienna; bequeathed by him to the Academy in 1821.

Gemäldegalerie der Akademie der bildenden Künste, Vienna

Rubens painted this *Adoration of the Shepherds* in 1608, during his stay in Italy, for the Oratorian church of San Filippo Neri at Fermo, which was consecrated in 1607. The grouping of the figures, and the light radiating from the Child, are inspired by Correggio's *Adoration of the Shepherds* at Dresden, which in Rubens's time was in the church of San Prospero at Reggio Emilia. Caravaggio's influence is seen in the sharp contrasts of light and shade and in the colour-scheme, which consists chiefly of brown tones.

In 1608-09, shortly after his return to Antwerp, Rubens repeated this composition in a large canvas of the same title which, however, is much freer and more powerful in style; it is now in St. Paul's church at Antwerp. See No. 127.

Canvas, 300 : 192 cm.

Bibl.:   R. Longhi, *La 'Notte' del Rubens a Fermo*, in *Vita Artistica*, II, 1927, pp. 191-7; L. Burchard, *Alcuni Dipinti del Rubens nel periodo italiano*, in *Pinacoteca*, I, 1928-29, pp. 1-2; L. Van Puyvelde, *Rubens' 'Aanbidding door de Herders' te Antwerpen*, in *Jaarboek van het Koninklijk Museum voor Schone Kunsten te Antwerpen*, 1942-7, pp. 83-7, M. Jaffé, *Rubens and the Oratorian Fathers*, in *Proporzioni*, IV, 1963, p. 209 e.v.

Prov.:   Church of San Filippo Neri, Fermo.

Museo Civico, Fermo

The angel appears to Mary as she is kneeling at a prie-dieu. She rises to her feet, one hand still on her prayer-book, the other raised in a gesture of surprise. The angel, kneeling on one knee, addresses her with reverence. The Holy Spirit descends towards Mary in a blaze of heavenly light; it is accompanied by five hovering cherubs, two of which scatter roses and lilies over the Virgin.

Rubens, who married Isabella Brant on 3 October 1609, was a member of the Antwerp 'Sodality of Married Men', an association run by the Jesuits and devoted to the Annunciation. He painted the present work for the Sodality in *c.* 1609-10. A preliminary oil sketch is in the Ashmolean Museum at Oxford (see No. 19).

Canvas, 224:200 cm.

Bibl.:   *Rooses*, I, pp. 185, 186, No. 143; *Oldenbourg*, pp. 91, 92; L. Burchard, *Skizzen des jungen Rubens*, in *Sitzungsberichte der kunstgeschichtlichen Gesellschaft Berlin*, 8 October 1926, p. 2, No. 6; *Glück*, p. 156; *Evers, 1943*, p. 206.

Prov.:   Professed House of the Jesuits at Antwerp; acquired thence in 1776 by the Empress Maria Theresa.

Kunsthistorisches Museum, Vienna

A preparatory oil sketch, ascribed to Rubens by L. Burchard, for
The Annunciation in Vienna (see No. 18). The latter work was painted
c. 1609-10 for the Married Men's Sodality in Antwerp.

Panel, 44:33 cm.

Bibl.: P. Buschmann, *Rubens en Van Dyck in het Ashmolean Museum te Oxford*,
in *Onze Kunst*, XXIX, 1916, pp. 8-13; *Catalogue of Paintings in the Ashmolean
Museum*, Oxford, s.a., p. 90, No. 380.

Prov.: Chambers Hall (Southampton and London, 1786-1855), who bequeathed it to
Oxford University.

The Ashmolean Museum, Oxford

Human hair plays an important role in magic and religion. Primitive men believed that the soul resided in all parts of the body; the hair was regarded as particularly important, and even as the main seat of vital strength. This is illustrated by the Biblical story of Samson and Delilah (*Judges*, 16:1-21): through Delilah's treachery Samson was made drunk and shorn so that he lost his great strength.

The painting shows the befuddled Samson lying at Delilah's feet, his head in her lap. A Philistine, aided by an old woman with a candle, is engaged in cutting off his hair; in the background two warriors stand in a doorway, waiting to overpower the helpless hero. A statue of Venus and Cupid in a niche recalls the love that brought about his overthrow.

This painting of *c.* 1610 belonged to Nicolaas Rockox, mayor of Antwerp and Rubens's friend and patron. Rockox died on 12 December 1640, and the work is mentioned in the inventory of his estate: "In the large parlour: An oil painting on panel, framed, representing Samson and Delilah, the work of Signor Rubens". Frans II Francken (1581-1642) depicted it above the fireplace in his painting of *Burgomaster Rockox's Art Gallery* in Munich.

A preparatory drawing by Rubens is in the collection of Professor I.Q. van Regteren Altena, Amsterdam (see No. 129), and a modello is in the Cincinnati museum.

Panel, 185 : 205 cm.

Bibl.:   L. Burchard, in *Glück*, p. 382; *Evers, 1943*, pp. 151-66; D. Rosen and J.S. Held, *A Rubens Discovery in Chicago*, in *The Journal of the Walters Art Gallery*, XIII-XIV, 1950-51, pp. 70-91, Cat. Exh. *Rotterdam, 1953-54*, pp. 37-9, under No. 6; *Burchard-d'Hulst*, 1956, pp. 46, 47, under No. 32; *Held*, p. 103, under No. 24; *Burchard-d'Hulst, 1963*, pp. 79, 80, under No. 46; Madlyn Kahr, *Delilah*, in *The Art Bulletin*, LIV, No. 3, 1972, pp. 295-7.

Prov.:   Nicolaas Rockox, mayor of Antwerp (d. 1640); Prince of Liechtenstein, Vienna; A. Neuerburg, Hamburg.

Private collection

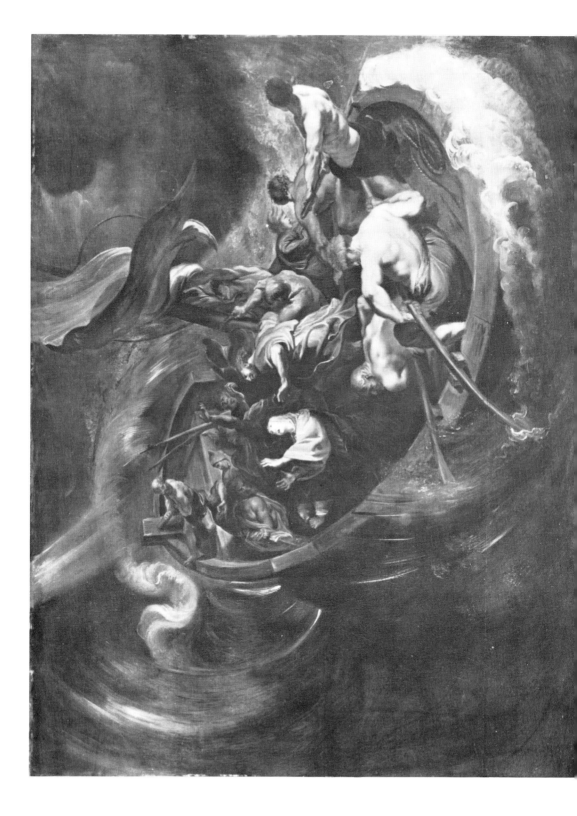

This painting illustrates a story first met with in the *Vita S. Walburgae* by Philipp von Rathsamhausen, Bishop of Eichstätt in Bavaria from 1306 to 1322. This author relates that the saint, who was of English origin, was crossing to Germany to help St. Boniface in his missionary work, when the ship was overtaken by a heavy storm. Thanks to St. Walburga's prayers the waves subsided and the ship was able to reach the shore.

This work is undoubtedly one of the three scenes that adorned the predella of the *Raising of the Cross* (commissioned in 1610) in St. Walburga's church at Antwerp, until they were replaced, between 1735 and 1737, by the new marble border by Willem Kerrickx. The whereabouts of the centre panel of the predella, representing *Christ's Death on the Cross*, and of the other side panel depicting *The Burial of St. Catherine*, are not at present known. However, the pedigree of *The Miracle of St. Walburga*, which was at one time in the collection of the painter Jacob de Wit, can be traced almost without interruption from St. Walburga's church to the Leipzig museum.

Panel, 75,5 : 98,5 cm.

Bibl.: S. Heiland, *Two Rubens Paintings rehabilitated*, in *The Burlington Magazine*, CXI, 1969, pp. 421-7.

Prov.: St. Walburga's church, Antwerp; purchased thence by Jacobus de Roore, The Hague; Jacob de Wit, Amsterdam; Johann Zacharias Richter (Leipzig, d. 1764); Johann Thomas Richter (Leipzig, 1728-83); Johann Friedrich Richter, sold at Leipzig in 1810; Fischer (artist), sold at Leipzig, 8 May 1820; Speck von Sternburg, Lützschena near Leipzig. In the Leipzig museum since 1945.

Museum der bildenden Künste, Leipzig, DDR

A fat satyr, drunk and asleep, lies in the foreground of a cave. One hand rests on his knee, the other on a panther lying beside him. The animal holds in its forepaws an overturned basket of grapes, a bunch of which is in its mouth. Behind the· satyr a young companion, his head wreathed with vine tendrils, is drinking the grape-juice that a nymph presses out into his goblet. At the satyr's feet, as if on a raised portion of the rocky floor, are vessels of all kinds including a richly chased tankard, a porcelain bowl, a nautilus goblet and many other implements. In the background, as if in a dream, a satyr is seen caressing a Bacchante.

In this painting, which can be dated on stylistic grounds *c*. 1610-11, Rubens holds up to the spectator a mirror of the animal passions and desires that beset humanity. The tableware is by another hand and is generally attributed to Frans Snijders.

Canvas, 158:217 cm.

Bibl.:   *Rooses*, III, pp. 95, 96, No. 611 bis; *Oldenbourg*, pp. 86, 87; R. Eigenberger, *Die Gemäldegalerie der Akademie der bildenden Künste in Wien*, Vienna-Leipzig, 1927, pp. 344-6; *Evers, 1943*, pp. 221-36.

Prov.: Count Anton Lamberg-Sprinzenstein, Vienna; bequeathed by him to the Academy in 1821.

Gemäldegalerie der Akademie der bildenden Künste, Vienna

Portrait of a robust, bearded man with dark hair; copied by Rubens *c.* 1610-12 after a portrait ascribed to Tintoretto (Venice, 1518-94) which was with the London art firm of Martin B. Asscher in 1950. The London portrait bore an unidentified coat of arms and the inscription ANO. ETATIS. SVE. XXXX, indicating that the sitter was forty years old. Rubens's painting was exhibited at Brussels in 1897 as a portrait of the Doge Cornaro, but the ground for this identification cannot be traced.

A woodcut after this portrait was made by Christoffel Jegher.

Panel, 59:48 cm.

Bibl.: *Rubens-Bulletijn*, V, 1897, p. 89; H. Hymans, *Une exposition de portraits anciens à Bruxelles dans les galeries du Musée moderne*, in *Gazette des Beaux-Arts*, 18, 1897, p. 81; E. Michel, *Rubens*, Paris, 1900, p. 291; Cat. Exh. *Kunstschatten. Twee Nederlandse collecties schilderijen uit de vijftiende tot en met de zeventiende eeuw en een collectie oud aardewerk*, Laren, 1959, No. 68; Mary L. Myers, *Rubens and the Woodcuts by Christoffel Jegher*, in *The Metropolitan Museum of Art Bulletin*, Summer 1966, pp. 7-23.

Prov.: Rousselle, exhibited at Brussels, 1897; Kleinberger, Paris, 1911; Leopold Koppel, Berlin, exhibited in 1914; Rosenberg & Stiebel, New York, 1951; Matthiesen Ltd, London.

M.P.W. Collection

After the iconoclastic riots of 1566 an *Adoration of the Shepherds* by Frans Floris was placed temporarily on the high altar of Our Lady's church at Antwerp to replace the destroyed triptych, also by Floris, the centre panel of which represented *The Coronation of the Virgin*. The church authorities sought to obtain a new altarpiece depicting the Assumption, and in 1611 two painters, Otto van Veen and Rubens, were asked to submit designs. Van Veen's has not survived, but one of the two sketches executed by Rubens as modelli has been preserved and is here exhibited; it belongs to the Hermitage in Leningrad.

The sketch falls into an upper and a lower part, depicting heaven and earth respectively. In the scene below, the stone has been rolled away from the Virgin's grave amid rocks, and the Apostles and holy women are amazed to find flowers in the empty tomb. Above, the Virgin is received into heaven, and Christ holds a wreath of roses over her head. For various reasons Rubens did not finally paint the altarpiece until 1625-27, by which time he had made new, modified sketches. A large painting on panel in the Vienna museum agrees with the present sketch as far as the lower half is concerned, but the upper part differs completely. There is good evidence to suggest that that painting was designed for the high altar of Our Lady's church, but for some reason was not used for its intended purpose.

Canvas, transferred to panel, 108 : 78 cm.

Bibl.:   *Rooses*, II, pp. 189, 190, No. 364; *Baudouin*, p. 55-9; C. Van de Velde, *Rubens' Hemelvaart van Maria in de Kathedraal te Antwerpen*, in *Jaarboek van het Koninklijk Museum voor Schone Kunsten*, Antwerp, 1975, pp. 252-9.

Prov.:   Acquired in 1770 at the F.I. Dufresne sale, Amsterdam.

Museum of the Hermitage, Leningrad

Sketch for the left panel of *The Deposition*, a triptych commissioned in 1611 by the Arquebusiers' Guild for their chapel in Our Lady's church in Antwerp. In the large painting the two women meet on a flight of steps, which does not appear in the sketch, and the poses are somewhat different. The steps and balustrade are borrowed from Veronese's picture of the same subject in the Barber Institute at Birmingham, while Rubens also gives evidence of having studied the work of Annibale Carracci. He was able, however, to subordinate these Italian influences to his own artistic personality.

A drawing in the Bonnat Museum at Bayonne comprises other studies for the Antwerp *Visitation* (see under No. 136).

Panel, 50 : 26 cm.

Bibl.: L. Burchard, *Skizzen des jungen Rubens*, in *Sitzungsberichte der kunstgeschichtlichen Gesellschaft Berlin*, October 1926-May 1927, p. 2, No. 14; Cat. Exh. *Rotterdam, 1953-54*, p. 42, No. 11; M. Jaffé, *Un chef-d'œuvre mieux connu*, in *L'Oeil*, 43-44, 1958, pp. 19, 20, 80.

Prov.: Acquired by W. von Bode on the London art market in 1890 for the Strasbourg museum.

Musée des Beaux-Arts, Strasbourg

Study 'from life' of the head of an aged man. Portrait studies of this kind are frequent in Rubens's early period and attest his admiration for robust male types with strong, expressive features. His use of bearded models for many of these heads reflects the baroque artist's delight in flowing lines and plastic forms with strong contrasts of light and shade.

Most of these studies were intended to be used as part of a composition; the present one is found in *The Woman Taken in Adultery*, c. 1612, now in Brussels.

The same head, engraved by Paul Pontius, occurs in a sheet of nine heads in a Drawing Book published at Antwerp by Petrus van Avont.

Panel, 67,3 : 50,2 cm.

Bibl.: A.P. de Mirimonde, *Une tête d'étude rubénienne au musée de Rouen*, in *Gazette des Beaux-Arts*, March 1960, pp. 151-54; *The Dayton Art Institute Bulletin*, 19, No. 4, January-February 1961, p. 1.

Prov.: Presented by Mr. and Mrs. Carlton W. Smith.

The Dayton Art Institute, Gift of Mr. and Mrs. Carlton W. Smith, Dayton, Ohio

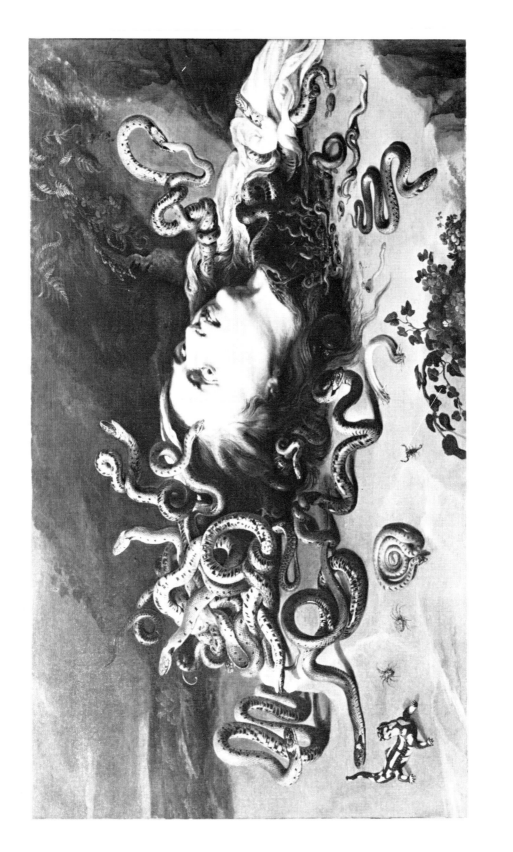

In Greek legend Medusa was one of the three Gorgons, frightful beings who punished with death anyone who looked upon their faces. In particular the head of Medusa, with serpents for hair, was associated with doom and terror. Perseus, the son of Jupiter and Danae, slew Medusa and presented her head to Minerva (Athene), who affixed it to her shield – the indestructible 'aegis', proof against lightning.

Medusa's severed head lies on a large stone. Some of the snakes have wriggled loose and are fighting one another, while others lie coiled up singly. New reptiles form out of the blood that pours from the neck, and little snakes creep forth out of isolated drops. A salamander and some insects can also be seen.

Medusa heads were depicted in antiquity and also by Leonardo da Vinci and Caravaggio. The smooth, careful execution indicates that Rubens painted this version soon after his return from Italy, probably *c.* 1612. The reptiles and insects are by another hand.

Canvas, 68,5 : 118 cm.

Bibl.: *K.d.K.*, p. 80; *Glück*, p. 162, No. 223; Cat. *Kunsthistorisches Museum, Wien, Verzeichnis der Gemälde*, Vienna, 1973, p. 147.

Prov.: Duke of Buckingham (cat. 1635, No. 21).

Kunsthistorisches Museum, Vienna

Venus fell in love with Adonis, a handsome young prince of Cyprus. Fearful of losing him, she urged him not to hunt dangerous animals; but the rash youth disregarded her advice, pursued a wild boar and was killed by it (Ovid, *Metamorphoses*, X, 525-739).

This scene does not show the fatal hunt or the boar, but Venus's lamentation over Adonis. The goddess crouches beside the body, splendid in form but already pale in death, and strokes the head of her beloved. Her three attendants (mentioned by other authors though not by Ovid) express their sorrow in convulsive gestures, while young Cupid, also weeping, unfastens his quiver as if to say that it is no use shooting love-arrows any more. The scene is completed by two hounds, one of which licks up Adonis's blood from the ground.

The academic classicism of this painting points to a date *c.* 1612-14. A preliminary oil sketch is in the Dulwich museum.

Canvas, 212:326 cm.

Bibl.:   *Smith, Catalogue Raisonné*, II, No. 751; *Rooses*, III, p. 179, No. 696; *Evers, 1943*, pp. 121-36; M. Jaffé, *The Death of Adonis by Rubens*, in *Duits Quarterly*, 11, 1967, pp. 3-16.

Prov.:   Bryan, sold in Pall Mall, London, 19 May 1798; Thomas Hope, sold at Christie's, London, 20 July 1917, lot 117, and bought there by Gooden and Fox for the first Lord Leverhulme; sold by his heirs at Christie's, London, 24 March 1961, and bought there by Mr. Duits.

Duits Ltd, London

The company of saints worshipping the Trinity is represented in the form of a vision. In the foreground, seen from behind, is St. Lawrence with his grid; St. Gregory is on the left, and on the right are the naked St. Sebastian and St. George in armour. In the distance is a group of monks led by St. Francis and St. Dominic. In the upper part of the sketch, in rather vague outline, the Virgin is seen standing on a cloud and facing towards the Trinity.

This composition was inspired by Titian's *Triumph of the Holy Trinity*, painted in 1554, which Rubens may have seen during his first visit to Spain in 1603; it was placed in the Escorial in 1574 and is now in the Prado. It may also be that he used as a model the engraving after Titian's work, executed by Cornelis Cort in 1566. The present sketch is not known to have served as a model for any painting, but the theme recurs in an engraving made before 15 May 1613 for the *Breviarium Romanum* published at Antwerp by Balthasar Moretus in 1614. The fact that the sketch is about four times as large as the engraving makes it unlikely that it was a design for the latter, but the resemblance between the two suggests a date of *c.* 1613 for the sketch. See No. 137.

Panel, 58 : 38 cm.

Bibl.:   L. Burchard, *Skizzen des jungen Rubens*, in *Sitzungsberichte der kunstgeschichtlichen Gesellschaft Berlin*, October 1926-May 1927, p. 3, No. 23; H.F. Bouchery and F. van den Wijngaert, *P.P. Rubens en het Plantijnsche Huis*, Antwerp-Utrecht, 1941, pp. 62, 132, 153; *Evers, 1943*, p. 219; Cat. Exh. *Rotterdam, 1953-54*, pp. 43, 44, No. 13; *d'Hulst, 1968*, pp. 90, 91, No. 3; *Vlieghe, Saints*, I, pp. 27, 28, No. 1.

Prov.:   Presented to the museum by A.J. Lamme in 1963.

Boymans-van Beuningen Museum, Rotterdam

The composition of this painting closely resembles a work by Parmi-gianino on a similar theme in the Vienna museum, which, according to Vasari, was painted in 1531 for Cavaliere Baiardi of Parma. Typical of Rubens are the putti, the modelling of Cupid and the light range of colouring that he generally used in 1614-18.

Rubens seldom signed or dated his works. This picture is one of the few exceptions: like *Venus frigida* in the Antwerp museum and *Susanna and the Elders* in the National Museum, Stockholm (see No. 33), it is signed and dated 1614.

Canvas, 142:108 cm. Signed and dated: *P.P. Rubens 1614.*

Bubl.:   *Rooses*, III, p. 69; *K.d.K.*, p. 72; L. van Puyvelde, *Les sources du style de Rubens*, in *Revue belge d'archéologie et d'histoire de l'art*, XXI, 1952, I, p. 31.

Prov.:   First recorded in the inventory of the *Residenz* at Munich, 1748.

Bayerische Staatsgemäldesammlungen, Munich

An illustration of the saying that Venus (goddess of love) is cold without Bacchus (god of wine) and Ceres (goddess of corn), i.e. that hunger and thirst are fatal to love. The adage is here treated positively, showing that love prospers when food and drink are abundant. A literal depiction of the theme can be found in Rubens's *Venus frigida*, painted in 1614 and now in the Antwerp museum. The present picture is notable for its academic classicism, and is one of a series of works of similar character executed *c.* 1612-15.

Canvas, 140,5 : 199 cm.

Bibl.: *Rooses*, III, p. 182, 183, No. 699; R. Oldenbourg, *Die Nachwirkung Italiens auf Rubens und die Gründung seiner Werkstatt*, in *Jahrbuch der Kunsthistorischen Sammlungen des allerhöchsten Kaiserhauses*, XXXIV, 1918, p. 193; Cat. *Staatliche Gemäldegalerie*, Kassel, 1958, p. 131, No. 85; W. Stechow, *Rubens and the Classical Tradition*, Cambridge, Mass., 1968, p. 48.

Prov.: Landgrave William VIII of Hesse, Kassel.

Staatliche Kunstsammlungen, Kassel

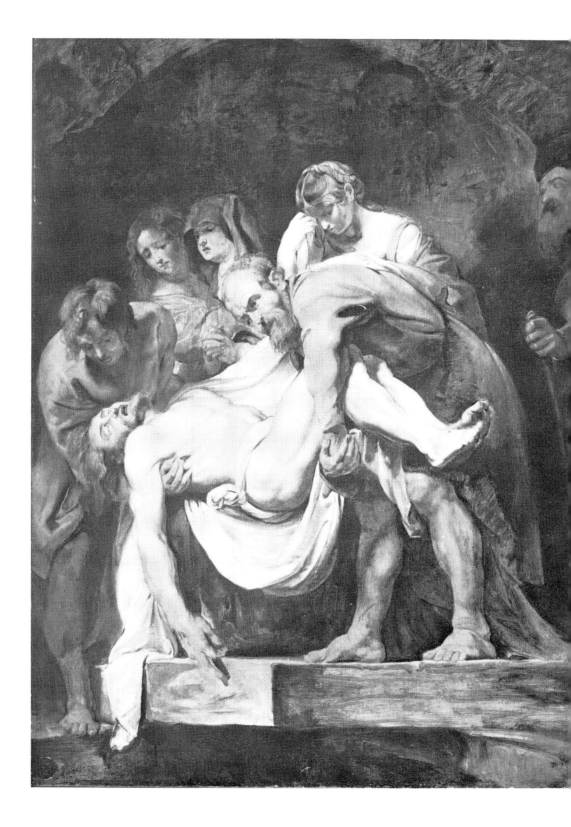

During his stay in Italy Rubens worked for the Chiesa Nuova in Rome and became acquainted with Caravaggio's *Entombment*, which was then in that church. The present work is a free interpretation of it, painted *c.* 1613-15 after Rubens's return to Antwerp. By eschewing the rhetorical gestures that Caravaggio had given some of the figures, he was able to comprise the whole group in a self-contained curve. Instead of hard isolated patches of colour he used graduated transitions, thus departing considerably from Caravaggio's style. In some places the brown, transparent priming can be clearly seen. See No. 139.

Panel, 88,3 : 66,5 cm.

Bibl.: *Smith, Catalogue Raisonné*, II, p. 104, No. 339; *Rooses*, II, pp. 136, 137, No. 323; A. von Schneider, *Caravaggio und die Niederländer*, Marburg a.d. Lahn, 1933, p. 96; R.H. Hubbard, *Catalogue of Paintings and Sculpture, The National Gallery of Canada*, I, Ottawa-Toronto, 1957, p. 67.

Prov.: Forchondt, Antwerp, 1710; Prince of Liechtenstein, Vienna, 1710. Acquired in 1956.

The National Gallery of Canada, Ottawa

Rubens painted the subject of *Susanna and the Elders* on several occasions (see No. 8). Its variety enabled him to display his talent to the full: landscape and interior, air and water, and the young, voluptuous nude contrasting with the senility of the Elders. As Rubens's own dating indicates, the Stockholm version was painted in 1614. Rubens's style at that time is evidenced by the way in which the smooth, glistening paint is applied, while the treatment of form is still intermediate between the classicism of the late sixteenth century and the full exuberance of baroque.

Panel, 66:51 cm. Signed and dated: *P.P. Rubens F. 1614.*

Bibl.: *K.d.K.*, p. 32; Cat. Exh. *Brussels, 1965*, pp. 170, 171, No. 183; Paola della Pergola, *P.P. Rubens e il tema della Susanna al bagno*, in *Bulletin van de Koninklijke Musea voor Schone Kunsten van België*, 1967, pp. 7-22.

Prov.: St. Luke's Guild, Antwerp, 1733; Louisa Ulrika, Queen of Sweden (1720-82); Gustavus III, King of Sweden (1746-92).

Nationalmuseum, Stockholm

The composition shows the Evangelists with their respective attributes. The three 'Synoptics' are seated at a table: St. Matthew listening to an angel, St. Mark with a lion and St. Luke with an ox. On the right, St. John looks up with inspired gaze towards an eagle.

The four Evangelists were depicted in a single painting by Correggio in 1521. The first Netherlands painter known to have treated the subject in this way is Frans Floris, in a lost composition known from an engraving of 1566.

This painting, clearly influenced by Caravaggio, was executed *c.* 1614. Some weaker parts, especially in the figures of Mark, Luke and the angel, suggest that it was done with help from the studio.

Canvas, 224:270 cm.

Bibl.:   *Rooses*, II, pp. 193, 194, No. 367; *Oldenbourg*, p. 104; E. Henschel-Simon, *Die Gemälde und Skulpturen der Bildergalerie von Sanssouci*, Berlin, 1950, No. 95; U. Moussalli, *Rubens et Caravage*, in *Études d'art publiées par le Musée d'Alger*, 11-2, 1955-6, p. 91; G. Eckardt, *Die Gemälde in der Bildergalerie von Sanssouci*, Potsdam, 1965, No. 83; *Vlieghe, Saints*, I, pp. 70-2, No. 54.

Prov.:   Purchased between 1755 and 1764 for the collection of Frederick II, King of Prussia.

Sanssouci, Bildergalerie, Potsdam

St. Augustine of Hippo, dressed in the habit of the Order named after him, is seen between Christ and the Virgin, kneeling on a small pile of books denoting his role as a Father of the Church. His mitre and crosier are on the ground before him.

The picture illustrates the apocryphal story that Augustine, presented with the choice of seeking refreshment in the blood of Christ or in Mary's milk, expressed his perplexity in the verse: *"Positus in medio, quo me vertam nescio, hic pascor a vulnere, hic lactor ab ubere."* His indecision is expressed in his features and bodily posture.

The figure of Christ is strongly influenced by the antique *Torso of a Faun*, which belonged to the Gaddi family at Florence until 1778 and is now in the Uffizi. The monumental and highly plastic treatment of the figures, the cool local colouring and the pronounced shadows point to a date of *c.* 1615.

Canvas, 237:179 cm.

Bibl.: *Rooses*, II, p. 220, No. 393; *K.d.K.*, p. 95; *Glück*, p. 157; A. Pérez Sanchez, *Real Academia de Bellas Artes de San Fernando. Inventario de las Pinturas*, Madrid, 1964, p. 63, No. 685; F. Labrada, *Real Academia de Bellas Artes de San Fernando, Catálogo de las Pinturas*, Madrid, 1965, p. 75, No. 685; *Vlieghe, Saints*, I, pp. 97, 98, No. 66.

Prov.: Jesuit college, Alcalá de Henares; transferred c. 1772 to the Jesuit college of San Isidoro at Madrid; deposited with the Academia de San Fernando at a date between 1829 and 1852.

Academia de San Fernando, Madrid

Ixion, who had been protected by Jupiter, ungratefully tried to seduce his consort Juno; but Jupiter outwitted him by the ruse shown in this picture. The scene is on Mount Olympus. On the left Ixion is embracing Juno's double Nephele, fashioned out of a cloud by Jupiter. Behind Ixion, and symbolizing his fate, is a Fury with a coil of snakes in her hand. Iris, the messenger of the gods, holds Juno's mantle over the pair: she is a party to the stratagem, as is shown by the fox's skin over her shoulder. Juno is seen on the right with her attribute, the peacock. She turns her back contemptuously on Ixion, and with one hand holds her hair in place: it has come loose because she has lent her diadem to Nephele. Cupid leads her by the hand to Jupiter, who is seen above with his eagle. On stylistic grounds the painting may be dated *c.* 1615.

Canvas, 171 : 245 cm.

Bibl.: *Smith, Catalogue Raisonné*, II, pp. 249, 250; *Rooses*, III, p. 111, No. 631; M. Rooses, *Vlaamsche kunst tentoongesteld ... te Brussel in 1910*, in *Onze Kunst*, XXIV, 1911, pp. 8, 9.

Prov.: Van de Amory, sold at Amsterdam in 1722; Sir Gregory Page Turner; Welbore Ellis Agar, sold at Christie's, London, 2 May 1806, lot 60; Duke of Westminster, London; Charles T. Yerkes, New York, sold at New York, 5-8 April 1910, lot 143. Bequeathed to the Louvre by Baron Basile de Schlichting in 1915.

Musée du Louvre, Paris

In 1224, two years before his death, St. Francis had a vision on Mount Alverna (La Verna) near Arezzo, where he was in retreat in the company of Brother Leo. The crucified Christ appeared to him in the form of a six-winged seraph, while the marks of the five wounds were miraculously imprinted on his hands, feet and side.

The picture shows St. Francis kneeling in a landscape and gazing ecstatically at the seraphic Christ, who appears before him in mid-air. His arms are outstretched in a gesture of humble submission, and the wounds in his hands are clearly visible. On the ground in front of him are a prayer-book, a crucifix and a skull, the *Vanitas* symbols appropriate to a hermit. Beside St. Francis can be seen the head of the startled Brother Leo.

The saint's oblique posture is typical of late Italian Mannerism. The painting was largely executed by Rubens's studio after a modello by him (now in the M.P.W. collection at Amsterdam), but the saint's head is by Rubens himself. The plastic treatment of the face and drapery points to a date *c.* 1615-20. See No. 38.

Canvas, 193,5 : 146 cm.

Bibl.: *Vlieghe, Saints*, I, pp. 142, 143, No. 91.

Prov.: Acquired after 1907.

Musée Municipal des Beaux-Arts, Arras

St. Francis of Assisi, kneeling on the ground, his arms outspread in ecstasy before the Seraphic Christ, receives the marks of the Saviour's five wounds.

An oil sketch in grey and brown tones, sober in technique and very direct in expression, for the picture of the same subject in the Musée Municipal at Arras, which may be dated *c.* 1615-20 on stylistic grounds (see No. 37).

Panel, 23,5 : 17,8 cm.

Bibl.:   J.S. Held, *A propos de l'exposition Rubens à Bruxelles*, in *Les Arts Plastiques*, VI, 2, 1953, p. 116; J. Müller Hofstede, *Neue Ölskizzen von Rubens*, in *Städel Jahrbuch*, N.F., II, 1969, pp. 213, 215, 216, 237; *Vlieghe, Saints*, I, p. 143, No. 91a.

Prov.:   Unknown German collection till 1932; Dr. Ludwig Burchard, Berlin, later London; Matthiesen Gallery, London.

M.P.W. Collection, Amsterdam

The Hero, in armour, embraces a naked, winged young woman who holds a laurel wreath above his head; she symbolizes the conquest of vice. The Hero shows his contempt for drunkenness by treading on a satyr, who lies prostrate beside a bunch of grapes; he also renounces lust, as is shown by Cupid weeping on Venus's shoulder. An old woman representing envy, with a tangle of snakes in her hair, flees in amazement and confusion.

As a pendant to this scene exalting virtue Rubens painted *The drunken Hercules*, an illustration of the effects of vice: the spectator was thus provided with models of conduct that should or should not be followed.

The original versions of *The crowning of the Hero* and *The drunken Hercules* are in the museums at Munich and Dresden respectively. They were painted *c.* 1612-14 and were very probably in Rubens's possession at his death. Both are on panel and in upright format.

The Dresden museum also possesses versions of both paintings executed partly by the studio; these, unlike the originals, are on canvas and in horizontal format, and on stylistic grounds they must be dated later, *c.* 1615-16. As the panels were not available on loan, we show here one of the canvases.

Canvas, 203 : 222 cm.

Bibl.:   *Smith, Catalogue Raisonné*, II, p. 83, No. 260; *Rooses*, IV, pp. 51, 52, No. 828; *K.d.K., ed. Rosenberg*, p. 18; E. Dillon, *Rubens*, London, 1909, pp. 82, 83, 94, 113, 132, 194; *K.d.K.*, pp. 456, 457 (under S. 56); E. Hensler, *Das Urbild des 'Trunkenen Hercules' von Rubens aufgefunden*, in *Kunstchronik*, 23-30 January 1926, pp. 662, 663; L. Burchard, *Zum Urbild des 'Trunkenen Hercules' von Rubens*, in *Kunstchronik*, 20-27 March 1926, pp. 763-5; *Evers, 1942*, pp. 174-79.

Prov.: Acquired in Mantua, 1743.

Staatliche Kunstsammlungen, Gemäldegalerie Alte Meister, Dresden, DDR

In this composition of half-length figures the sexes are separated. Diana stands on the right, with a spear in her hand and dead game in her tucked-up garment; behind her are three nymphs, and on the other side three satyrs. One of these holds out a rich variety of fruit, while another has a basket of fruit on his head and offers a bunch of grapes to one of the nymphs. Not only are the sexes opposed to each other, but Diana's seriousness and the chaste innocence of the nymphs contrast with the animal exuberance of the satyrs: one side of the picture is spiritual, the other physical.

In view of the style, the work may be dated *c.* 1616. The dog, the game and the fruit are by Frans Snijders.

Canvas, 136:182 cm.

Bibl.: *Rooses*, III, p. 79, 80, No. 597; R. Oldenbourg, *Die Nachwirkung Italiens auf Rubens und die Gründung seiner Werkstatt*, in *Jahrbuch der Kunsthistorischen Sammlungen des allerhöchsten Kaiserhauses*, XXXIV, 1918, p. 201 e.a.; *Glück*, p. 160 (No. 133), 360, 395; *Evers, 1942*, p. 196 e.a.

Prov.: Purchased by Raschke at Antwerp in 1710.

Staatliche Kunstsammlungen, Gemäldegalerie Alte Meister, Dresden, DDR

In the seventeenth century it was not uncommon for famous artists, who mostly specialized in particular genres, to collaborate in producing a picture. The present work is the result of co-operation between two great masters who were also personal friends: the medallion of the Virgin is by Rubens, while the floral border and the wreath above her head are by Jan I Breughel. The latter wrote as follows on 5 September 1621 to Ercole Bianchi, the agent of Cardinal Federigo Borromeo, Archbishop of Milan; "… I send you another painting, the finest and most exquisite piece I have done in my life. Signor Rubens has also displayed his talent in the medallion, in which is a very fine Madonna. The birds and other creatures are painted from life, after specimens in the possession of the illustrious Infanta." The picture must have been finished by the end of 1617 at latest, as it figures in *Sight*, one of five paintings illustrating the senses, executed by Breughel with staffage by Rubens, and that work (now in the Prado at Madrid) bears the date *1617*.

Panel transferred to canvas, 85:65 cm.

Bibl.: *Smith, Catalogue Raisonné*, II, p. 115, No. 390; *Rooses*, I, pp. 204-6, No. 199; Cat. Exh. *Rubens et son temps*, Paris, 1936, No. 65; Cat. Exh. *De Madonna in de Kunst*, Antwerp, 1954, p. 134, No. 93; M.L. Hairs, *Les peintres flamands de fleurs au XVIIe siècle*, Paris-Brussels, 1955, pp. 29, 30, 153, 202.

Prov.: Cardinal Federigo Borromeo, Archbishop of Milan, 1621; Biblioteca Ambrosiana, Milan; in Paris since 1796.

Musée du Louvre, Paris

The picture shows carriers returning at nightfall from a quarry, their cart laden with stones. They descend laboriously with their heavy burden towards a ford; the horse has just set his forefeet on the marshy ground. The landscape is mountainous, and in the centre is a rock partly overgrown with trees and bushes, giving access to a cave. On the left-hand slope of the rock a man and woman are warming themselves by a fire.

This landscape was probably painted *c.* 1617. See No. 92.

Canvas transferred to panel, 86 : 126,5 cm.

Bibl.: *Smith, Catalogue Raisonné,* II, p. 157, No. 547; *Idem,* IX, p. 303, No. 216; *Rooses,* IV, pp. 369, 370, No. 1178; G. Glück, *Die Landschaften von Peter Paul Rubens,* Vienna, 1945, p. 56, No. 7.

Prov.: Probably Cardinal Mazarin, Paris; Earl Cadogan; Sir Robert Walpole, Houghton Hall; acquired from him in 1779 by Catherine II of Russia.

Museum of the Hermitage, Leningrad

q. v. Dutch + Flemish Ptgs from the Hermitage pp. 104-5

The Virgin, with the Child Jesus on her lap, is seated on a cloud, surrounded by a crowd of small children which form a kind of wreath as they circle round her. Two of them hold a crown over her head, and two others, above on the right, carry palms. The children are not winged and therefore cannot be regarded as cherubs. Most probably they represent the souls of the Holy Innocents massacred at Bethlehem, whose feast is celebrated on 28 December. On stylistic grounds the picture may be dated *c.* 1618.

Canvas, 138:100 cm.

Bibl.: *Smith, Catalogue Raisonné*, II, p. 116; *Rooses*, I, pp. 269, 270, No. 204; *K.d.K.*, p. 197; L. Hourticq, *Rubens*, Paris, 1924, p. 79.

Prov.: Collection of Louis XIV, King of France.

Musée du Louvre, Paris

The scene is based on the well-known legend of the twins Romulus and Remus and the foundation of Rome. Sons of the god Mars by the Vestal Virgin Rhea Silvia, who was under a vow of chastity, they and their mother were thrown into the Tiber by Amulius, king of Alba Longa. Rhea Silvia was rescued by the river god Tiberinus, who made her his wife. The basket carrying the children was swept downstream and eventually washed ashore. The babes were found by a she-wolf, which suckled them until a shepherd, Faustulus, discovered them and took them into his home. On the left of the picture are Rhea Silvia and the river-god Tiberinus, leaning on a large pitcher with water streaming out of it; the herdsman Faustulus is running up from the right. The painting was executed at Antwerp, *c.* 1618.

Canvas, 210 : 212 cm.

Bibl.:   *Smith, Catalogue Raisonné*, II, p. 152, No. 532; *Rooses*, IV, pp. 16, 17, No. 801; *Glück*, p. 158, 392; *Van Puyvelde*, p. 115.

Prov.:   Probably in Rubens's estate at his death; belonged to Cardinal Pio di Carpi, also called di Savoia (1612-39), and was sold by his great-nephew, Prince Gilberto Pio di Savoia, to Benedict XIV, Pope from 1740 to 1758 and founder of the Capitoline collection.

Museo Capitolino, Rome

Michiel Ophovius, born in 1571 at 's Hertogenbosch (Bois-le-Duc), entered the Dominican monastery of St. Paul at Antwerp in 1585. In 1626, at the instance of the Infanta Isabella, he became bishop of his native city. He moved to Antwerp when 's Hertogenbosch was captured by the Dutch in 1629, and died at Lier on 4 November 1637.

Ophovius, wearing the Dominican habit, gestures as though addressing the spectator. He is a robust-looking man with a massive head and small eyes glittering with shrewdness and will-power. The portrait dates from *c.* 1618.

Another version, in a private collection in Brussels, is of no less quality than this one.

Canvas, 111.5 : 82.5 cm.

Bibl.: *Rooses*, IV, pp. 226, 227, No. 1013; *K.d.K.*, p. 167; *Beknopte catalogus van de schilderijen, beeldhouwwerken en miniaturen*, Mauritshuis, The Hague, 1968, p. 125, No. 252; H. Vlieghe, *Portraits II, Corpus Rubenianum Ludwig Burchard*, XIX (in preparation).

Prov.: Dominican monastery, Antwerp; Vinck de Wesel sale, Antwerp, 27 April 1813; Stier d'Aertselaer sale, Antwerp, 1822.

Koninklijk Kabinet van Schilderijen 'Mauritshuis', The Hague

Probably executed *c.* 1620, this work was still in Rubens's possession at his death, when it was inventoried as '*la pucelle d'Orléans*'.

The armoured Maid kneels before a crucifix, praying for victory in the coming battle. She has taken off her plumed helmet and laid her iron gauntlets on the floor. Her attitude is calm and serene, and her features, despite their simplicity, express great spiritual power and heroism.

This picture of Joan, one of the few known to us from the seventeenth or eighteenth century, is probably based on a woodcut reproducing one of the two sixteenth-century monuments erected in her honour on the bridge at Orleans.

Canvas, 181.6 : 116.2 cm.

Bibl.: Johanna Schopenhauer, *Ausflug an den Niederrhein und Belgiën*, I, Leipzig, 1831, p. 221; *Rooses*, IV, pp. 31, 32, No. 816; W. Valentiner, *Joan of Arc by Rubens*, in *North Carolina Museum of Art Bulletin*, I, 3, 1957, pp. 11-16.

Prov.: In the artist's possession; J.B. Cachiopin, Antwerp, 1662; A.J.A. Schaffhausen, Cologne; Sibilla von Wittgenstein; D. Hjorth, Malmö, Sweden; Baron von Platen, Sweden.

The North Carolina Museum of Art; original state appropriation and gift of the North Carolina Art Society (Robert E. Phifer Funds), Raleigh, North Carolina

Alatheia, daughter of Gilbert Talbot, Earl of Shrewsbury, married in 1606 Thomas Howard, Earl of Arundel and one of the most famous English art-lovers.

Three portraits of the Earl by Rubens are known; these are respectively in the Isabella Stewart Gardner Museum at Boston (see under No. 161), the National Gallery and the National Portrait Gallery, London (see No. 82). Rubens also painted a portrait, now at Munich, of the Countess without her husband, but with friends who accompanied her to Antwerp in 1620, on the way from The Hague to Brussels (see under No. 153). Van Dyck painted a portrait of the Earl and Countess which is also now at Munich.

It appears from an inventory of 1646 that Rubens's brother-in-law, the Antwerp silk merchant and tapestry dealer Peter van Hecke the Younger, possessed "two portraits by Rubens of the Earl and Countess of Arundel". The entry indicates that there were two separate pictures, and the present portrait of Alatheia Talbot may be one of them. It shows her in approximately the same pose as in the large painting of 1620 in Munich; whether that is an autograph work by Rubens has, however, never been thoroughly investigated.

Canvas, 107:78 cm.

Bibl.: *Smith, Catalogue Raisonné*, IX, pp. 340, 341, No. 362; F.J. Sanchez Canton, *La collection Cambó*, Barcelona, 1935, pp. 94-6; E. Duverger, *De verzameling schilderijen van de Antwerpse zijde- en tapijthandelaar Peter van Hecke de Jonge, schoonbroer van P.P. Rubens, naar een inventaris van 1646*, in *Jaarboek van het Koninklijk Museum voor Schone Kunsten*, Antwerp, 1971, pp. 151-3; *Huemer, Portraits I*, under No. 4.

Prov.: Presented to the museum by Sr. Cambó.

Museo de Arte de Cataluña, Barcelona

St. Gregory of Nazianze, Allbright-Knox Art Gallery, Buffalo

THE CEILING PAINTINGS FOR THE FORMER JESUIT CHURCH AT ANTWERP

On 29 March 1620 Rubens signed a contract with Jacobus Tirinus, head of the Professed House of the Jesuits, by which he undertook to deliver within a year 39 paintings for the ceilings of the side-aisles and galleries of the church. A preliminary list of subjects was to be supplied to him, and for each painting he was to do a small sketch in his own hand. The execution might be entrusted to his assistants, Van Dyck being expressly mentioned, but Rubens promised "in honour and conscience" that he would "remedy with his own hand whatever might be found amiss."

The greater part of the interior of the church was ravaged by fire on 18 July 1718, and all the ceiling paintings, which were on linen, were destroyed. However, many of Rubens's oil sketches have been preserved (see Nos. 48-55).

Thanks to various paintings of the church interior we are able to form an idea of the brilliant decorative effect; this is aided a.o. by drawings made in the church after Rubens's paintings in 1711-12 by the painter Jacob de Wit (1695-1754).

Oil sketch for "Sanctus Basilius", the fourth ceiling painting in the list attached to Rubens's contract with Jacobus Tirinus, the Jesuit superior at Antwerp (see p. 119).

Although St. Basil was bishop of Caesarea he is here dressed as a monk. The pillar on the left represents the pillar of fire with which legend associates him. He is seen kneeling on clouds, with his face raised to heaven and his arms outspread in a gesture of entreaty. His pose may be compared with that of St. Ignatius praying for the sick in the great altarpiece in the church of Sant' Ambrogio at Genoa, painted by Rubens only a few months before.

Panel, 50:64.8 cm.

Bibl.:   *Rooses*, I, p. 33, No. 21bis; *Van Puyvelde, Esquisses*, p. 26; *Martin, Ceiling Paintings*, pp. 130, 131, No. 21a.

Prov.:   Burtin, Brussels; purchased from him in 1801 by Duke Ernest II of Gotha-Altenburg; Ducal Museum, Gotha.

Schlossmuseum, Gotha, DDR

The list attached to Rubens's contract with Jacobus Tirinus, superior of the Antwerp Jesuits, mentions as the tenth ceiling painting an "Annunciatio B. V^{is}". Rubens made several sketches for this subject, of which two have survived, a grisaille on panel in the Ashmolean Museum at Oxford and the present modello from the Vienna Academy. The oval form of the composition and the *di sotto in su* perspective indicate the purpose for which it was intended. Subsequently, however, the plan was modified and this subject was rejected; the final decision, moreover, was for rectangular or octagonal compositions. See p. 119.

Panel, 31.8:44 cm.

Bibl.:   *Rooses*, I, p. 41, No. 40; *K.d.K.*, p. 212; *Van Puyvelde, Esquisses*, pp. 26, 74; *Martin, Ceiling Paintings*, pp. 189, 190, No. 40 (II)b.

Prov.:   Anonymous sale at Brussels from 18 July 1740, lot 268; J. de Roore (1686-1747), sold at The Hague from 4 September 1747, lot 43; Anthoni and Stephanus de Groot, sold at The Hague, 20 March 1771, lot 6; Count Anton Lamberg-Sprinzenstein (1740-1822), who presented it to the Vienna Academy in 1821.

Gemäldegalerie der Akademie der bildenden Künste, Vienna

The list attached to Rubens's contract with Jacobus Tirinus, superior of the Antwerp Jesuits, mentioned as the eleventh ceiling painting a "Nativitas X^i" (see p. 119). In the present oil sketch for this subject the arrangement of the figures recalls an earlier *Adoration of the Shepherds* by Rubens, of which one version is at Fermo in Italy and another in St. Paul's church in Antwerp. A comparison of the sketch with these works shows clearly what alterations of perspective were required for a ceiling painting and how skilfully Rubens achieved these, apparently without any resort to technical tricks.

The sketch shows several *pentimenti*, e.g. in the figure of the old woman crouching by the crib. Rubens first painted her with hands outstretched in a gesture of wonder, but he then changed his mind and made her clasp her hands in prayer.

Panel, 32 : 47.8 cm.

Bibl.: *Rooses*, I, p. 21, No. 2bis; *K.d.K.*, ed. *Rosenberg*, p. 194; *Van Puyvelde, Esquisses*, p. 27; *Martin, Ceiling Paintings*, pp. 60-2, No. 2a.

Prov.: Victor Wolfvoet (Antwerp, 1612-52)?; Joseph Sansot, sold at Brussels, 20 July 1739, lot 125; anonymous sale, Brussels, 18 July 1740, lot 267; J. de Roore, sold at The Hague from 4 September 1747, lot 44; Anthoni and Stephanus de Groot, sold at The Hague, 20 March 1771, lot 7; Count Anton Lamberg-Sprinzenstein (1740-1822), who presented it to the Vienna Academy in 1821.

Gemäldegalerie der Akademie der Bildenden Künste, Vienna

The list attached to Rubens's contract with Jacobus Tirinus, superior of the Antwerp Jesuits, mentioned as the sixteenth ceiling painting a "Resurrectio Chⁱ" (see p. 119). The present oil sketch of this subject was discovered as recently as 1974 by Jacques Foucart in the storeroom of the Dijon museum. Stylistically it closely resembles previously known sketches for this cycle, which display in a similar fashion Rubens's virtuosity and highly personal style.

Panel, 24.5 : 19.7 cm.

Bibl.:   *Martin, Ceiling Paintings*, p. 96, No. 12a; J. Foucart, *Une Esquisse de Rubens retrouvée à Dijon*, in *La Revue du Louvre*, 1974, pp. 19-24, No. 1.

Prov.:   Presented to the Dijon museum by Jules Maciet in 1904.

Musée des Beaux-Arts, Dijon

An oil sketch, one of the preparatory works for "Sanctus Augustinus", the twenty-fourth item in the list of ceiling paintings attached to Rubens's contract with Jacobus Tirinus, superior of the Antwerp Jesuits (see p. 119).

From surviving copies of the final painting it appears to have conformed in the main to the present sketch. St. Augustine, in bishop's robes, kneels in ecstasy, gazing up to heaven with arms outstretched. In his right hand he holds a heart transfixed by an arrow: "Thou hadst pierced our hearts with Thy charity" (*Confessions,* IX, 3). Divine love was more to the Saint than theological learning and episcopal dignity: thus we see books, scrolls and a crosier lying unheeded in a corner, while a playful cherub crowns himself with the mitre.

Panel, 48:64 cm.

Bibl.:   *Rooses,* I, p. 37, No. 30bis; *Van Puyvelde, Esquisses,* p. 27; *Martin, Ceiling Paintings,* p. 158, No. 30a.

Prov.:   Burtin, Brussels; bought from him in 1801 by Ernest II, Duke of Gotha-Altenburg; Ducal Museum, Gotha; E. & A. Silberman Galleries, New York.

Stiftung Sammlung E.G. Bührle, Zürich

Noah is seen offering a sacrifice of thanksgiving to God after the deluge (*Genesis*, 8:20). He kneels in the centre of the picture, his arms upraised in prayer, before an altar on which the carcase of an animal lies. Two of his sons prepare the sacrifice; one arranges the firewood on the altar, while the other is about to slaughter a sheep. Noah's wife is seen as an old woman in prayer. Three other members of his family stand behind him.

This grisaille sketch, which has been considerably damaged, was a design for a ceiling painting for the former Jesuit church in Antwerp (see p. 119). It was followed by a modello. The subject, however, does not figure in the list attached to the contract signed by Rubens. Probably the two sketches were executed when the original programme was being revised and before the definitive list of subjects was drawn up. At all events, *Noah's Sacrifice* was not among the ceiling paintings that eventually adorned the church.

Panel, 19:29 cm.

Bibl.: P. Buschmann, *Rubens en Van Dyck in het Ashmolean Museum te Oxford*, in *Onze Kunst*, XXIX, 1916, pp. 18-20; *Van Puyvelde, Esquisses*, p. 27; *Catalogue of Paintings in the Ashmolean Museum*, Oxford, s.a., p. 90, No. 384; E. Haverkamp Begemann, *De kroning van Maria*, in *Bulletin Museum Boymans*, VIII, 1957, p. 83, n. 4; *Martin, Ceiling Paintings*, p. 193, No. 40 (IV)a.

Prov.: Maximiliaan de Hase, sold at Brussels from 10 June 1782, lot 5?; Count de Cuypers de Reymenam, sold at Brussels, 27 April 1802, lot 114?; Charles Spruyt (1769-1851), sold at Ghent from 28 July 1806, lot 166; sold at Ghent from 3 October 1815, lot 131; Thomas Loridon de Ghellinck, sold at Ghent from 3 September 1821, lot 216; Chambers Hall (Southampton and London, 1786-1855), who bequeathed it to Oxford University.

Ashmolean Museum, Oxford

St. Lucy of Syracuse, whose feast-day is December 13, was tortured and condemned to be burnt for her Christian faith; when the flames spared her, an enraged executioner stabbed her with a dagger. She is shown in a white and blue garment of a delicate shade, as a symbol of purity. Another virgin martyr, St. Agatha, descends from heaven, holding a palm-branch in one hand and extending the other protectively over Lucy's head.

A modello for one of the ceiling paintings for the former Jesuit church at Antwerp (see p. 119). The list of subjects attached to the contract signed by Rubens included as No. 30: "Sancta Lucia cum Sᵃ Agatha illi apparente".

Panel, 30,5 : 46 cm.

Bibl.:   *Van Puyvelde, Esquisses*, pp. 27, 75, 76, No. 37; F. Baudouin, *Nota's bij de tentoonstelling 'Schetsen en tekeningen van P.P. Rubens'*, in *Bulletin Koninklijke Musea voor Schone Kunsten, Brussel*, II, 1953, p. 50; *Martin, Ceiling Paintings*, pp. 155, 156, No. 29b.
Prov.:   Count de Silgay, who bequeathed it to the museum in 1862.

Musée Municipal des Beaux-Arts, Quimper

According to the *Golden Legend* Barbara, daughter of the satrap Dioscurus, aroused the wrath of her pagan father by ambracing Christianity. The painting shows him pursuing her up the steps of a terrace. On the left is the tower in which he afterwards imprisoned her for long years as a punishment.

A grisaille oil sketch, the first compositional design for one of the ceiling paintings in the former Jesuit church at Antwerp. "Sancta Barbara" figures as No. 15 in the list of subjects attached to the contract between Rubens and the Jesuit superior Jacobus Tirinus (see p. 119). The final painting differed little from this sketch.

Panel, 15 : 21 cm.

Bibl.: P. Buschmann, *Rubens en Van Dyck in het Ashmolean Museum te Oxford*, in *Onze Kunst*, XXIX, 1916, pp. 17, 18; *Van Puyvelde, Esquisses*, pp. 26, 74, 75, No. 33; *Catalogue of Paintings in the Ashmolean Museum*, Oxford, s.a., p. 90, No. 382; *Martin, Ceiling Paintings*, pp. 160, 161, No. 31a.

Prov.: Maximiliaan de Hase, sold at Brussels from 10 June 1782?; Count de Cuypers de Reymenam, sold at Brussels, 27 April 1802?; Charles Spruyt (1769-1851), sold at Ghent from 28 July 1806, lot 171; sold at Ghent from 3 October 1815; Thomas Loridon de Ghellinck, sold at Ghent, 3 September 1821, lot 214; Chambers Hall (Southampton and London, 1786-1855), who bequeathed it to Oxford University.

Ashmolean Museum, Oxford

An oil sketch in grisaille, executed *c.* 1620-21 for the crowning of the high altar of the former Jesuit church, now dedicated to St. Charles Borromeo, in Antwerp. Rubens painted two imposing pictures of *St. Ignatius Loyola* and *St. Francis Xavier* for this church (both now in Vienna) and also designed a portico for the high altar, in which the pictures were to be displayed alternately. Besides the present sketch, drawings for the architecture and sculpture of this portico have survived (see No. 149). The sketch is to be regarded as an advanced preliminary study, but the portico as finally executed bears only a general resemblance to it.

Panel, 55.9 : 76.2 cm.

Bibl.: *Goris-Held*, p. 34, under No. 56; Nina Ayala Mallory, *El altar mayor en la iglesia de San Ignacio de Amberes*, in *Goya*, 79, Madrid, July-August, 1967, pp. 2-13; F. Baudouin, *De datering van twee schilderijen van Rubens voor het hoofdaltaar van de Antwerpse Jezuëtenkerk en enkele aantekeningen over Hans van Mildert*, in *Miscellanea Jozef Duverger*, Gent, 1967, pp. 314, 315, No. 60.

Prov.: A. de Groot, The Hague, 1748; Vanderstraelen-Moons-Van Lerius sale, Antwerp, 1885; J.-B. Foucart, sold at Valenciennes, 12-14 October 1898, lot 93; Dr. A. Jaffé, Berlin; art firm of W.E. Duits, London.

Private collection

The *Charites* of Greek mythology were known to the Romans as Graces *(Gratiae)*. Originally perhaps goddesses of the earth and of fertility, they came to signify beauty (Aglaia), joy (Euphrosyne) and festivity or abundance (Thalia). They were depicted in earlier times as draped but later as naked, in a group with arms intertwined.

Rubens treated this subject more than once. The present version is a grisaille sketch for a small cylindrical high relief, probably in ivory, which, however, has not been traced. A drawn copy, now in the Copenhagen museum, is based on another composition sketch for the same work. The present sketch may be dated *c.* 1620-23 on stylistic grounds.

Canvas, 47.5 : 35 cm.

Bibl.: *Smith, Catalogue Raisonné*, II, p. 150, No. 522; *Rooses*, III, pp. 99, 100, No. 615; *K.d.K.*, p. 223.

Prov.: Presented in 1671 by Mgr. Airoldi, internuncio in Brussels, to Cardinal Leopold de' Medici in Rome.

Galleria Palatina, Palazzo Pitti, Florence

The identification of this subject with Rubens's first wife is based chiefly on the resemblance to Van Dyck's *Portrait of Isabella Brant in front of the portico of Rubens's house* in the National Gallery, Washington. Rubens married Isabella in 1609; she was born in 1591 and died suddenly on 20 June 1626, apparently of the plague. It was doubtless a heavy blow to Rubens, who wrote to Pierre Dupuy on 15 July: "I have in truth lost a very good companion ... having none of the vices usual in her sex. She was all goodness and amiability ..." The memory of Rubens's first wife remains vivid owing to his numerous portraits of her alone or (as in the Alte Pinakothek, Munich) the two of them together. All of these show her as a sweet-natured figure with large, lively eyes and a delicate nose, a smile on her unparted lips. The portrait seen here was painted *c.* 1620-25.

Panel, 53 : 46 cm.

Bibl.: *Rooses-Ruelens*, III, pp. 444-7, No. 404; W. von Bode, *Ein neuaufgefundenes Bildnis von Rubens' erster Gattin Isabella Brant*, in *Jahrbuch des Königlich Preuszischen Kunstsammlungen*, XXXV, 1914, pp. 221-3; *Glück*, pp. 96, 97, 384, 385; *Goris-Held*, p. 26, No. 1; H.S. Francis, *Portrait of Issabella Brant by Peter Paul Rubens*, in *The Bulletin of the Cleveland Museum of Art*, XXXIV, 1947, pp. 247-9; H. Vlieghe, *Portraits II, Corpus Rubenianum Ludwig Burchard*, XIX (in preparation).

Prov.: Lord Glanusk, sold at Sotheby's, London, 1914; Hugh Blaker, Old Isleworth, Middlesex; Marcus Keppel, sold by Paul Cassirer, Berlin, 1930; private collection, New York.

The Cleveland Museum of Art, Mr. and Mrs. William H. Marlatt Fund, 1947, Cleveland, Ohio

Susanna (1599-1643) was the third daughter of Daniel Fourment, a silk-merchant and tapestry dealer in Antwerp, and of his wife Clara Stappaert. She married Raymond del Monte in 1617, and subsequently Arnold Lunden in 1622. Her youngest sister, Helena, became Rubens's wife in 1630.

The portrait of Susanna in the National Gallery in London has been known as the *'chapeau de paille'* since the late eighteenth century – wrongly, as it shows her wearing a plumed beaver hat. The sobriquet would, however, be appropriate to the present painting of *c.* 1620-25, which was called *'portrait de Susanne Fourment en bergère'* in an inventory of works of art belonging to the Lunden family: she is seen wearing a straw hat and holding a crook, and over her shoulder is the strap of her satchel.

The confusion of titles is not surprising, as Rubens painted numerous portraits of Susanna Fourment: no less than four were in his possession at his death.

Panel, 68 : 58 cm.

Bibl.: G.P. Mensaert, *Le peintre amateur et curieux*, I, Brussels, 1763, pp. 196-8, 260; *Smith, Catalogue Raisonné*, II, p. 261, No. 882; *Idem*, IX, p. 272, No. 103; *Rooses*, IV, pp. 175-9 (under No. 949), 182 (under No. 953); L. Burchard in *Glück*, p. 389; G. Martin, *National Gallery Catalogues, The Flemish School, c. 1600-c. 1900*, London, 1970, pp. 174-82, under No. 852; H. Vlieghe, *Une grande collection anversoise du dix-septième siècle: le cabinet d'amateur d'Arnold Lunden, beau-frère de Rubens*, in *Jahrbuch der Berliner Kunstsammlungen*, 1977 (in print).

Prov.: Mentioned as belonging to the Lunden family in an inventory drawn up between 1639 and 1644; Arnold-Willem-Jozef Lunden (1732-82); owned in 1785 by the Antwerp art firm of Pilaer and Beeckemans; Stier d'Aertselaer; Schamp d'Aveschoot, Ghent, on sale there in 1840, lot C, but withdrawn; private collection, Brussels.

Private collection

Modello for a tapestry, one of a series of twelve depicting *The History of the Emperor Constantine*, commissioned by King Louis XIII of France probably at the beginning of 1622. The theme was a popular one in the seventeenth century, affording an indirect means of glorifying living sovereigns. The sketches were completed by the end of 1622 or beginning of 1623. The tapestries were woven in the Paris studio of Marc de Comans and Frans van der Plancken, actual-size cartoons being first made on the basis of Rubens's sketches.

Roma is seated in the centre on a throne under a baldachin; her left hand rests on a globe, while in the other she holds a small figure of Victory. A winged genius holding a palm-branch places a crown on her head; beside her is a second genius with the standards of conquered armies. Constantine stands on the right with three captives at his feet; he is in armour and holds in his hand a thunder-bolt, the weapon and attribute of Jupiter, to whom he is thus likened. On the left are two captive barbarian chiefs. In the foreground Romulus and Remus, suckled by the she-wolf, allude to the founda-tion of Rome. This oil sketch was preceded by a drawing now in the Albertina at Vienna, in which only the main figures appear.

Panel, 54:69 cm.

Bibl.: *Rooses*, III, pp. 201, 213, 214, Nos. 713 and 724; *Rubens-Bulletijn*, V, p. 306; *Van Puyvelde, Esquisses*, pp. 27-9, No. 7; *Burchard*, pp. 20-2; Cat. Exh. *Rotterdam, 1953-54*, p. 63, No. 41; *Burchard-d'Hulst, 1963*, pp. 208-11, under No. 133; *d'Hulst, 1968*, p. 96, No. 14.

Prov.: Marc de Comans and Frans van der Plancken, Paris; Hippolyte de Comans, Paris; Philippe, duc d'Orléans (d. 1727); 'Philippe Égalité', who sold it in 1792 to Thomas Moore Slate, London; De Calonne, sold in London, 23-28 March 1795?; Earl of Liverpool, sold in London, 25 May 1829, lot 64; Sir J.C. Robinson (London, 1824-1913); Sir Francis Cook, Richmond; D. and N. Katz, Dieren, Gelderland (1940) and Basle, who presented it to the Mauritshuis in 1947.

Koninklijk Kabinet van Schilderijen 'Mauritshuis', The Hague

Study of an unknown man with long hair, moustache and beard, looking to the right at an object outside the picture. Light falls from the right, casting deep shadows on the side of his face that is turned towards the spectator. The dramatic effect of the pose and illumination suggests strongly that Rubens painted the head from life, intending to use it in one or other of his great compositions. A very similar figure occurs in *The Adoration of the Magi*, now in the Antwerp museum.

This study, engraved by Paul Pontius, appears in a sheet of nine heads in a Drawing-Book published at Antwerp by Petrus van Avont.

Panel, 50:42 cm.

Bibl.: *Rooses*, V, pp. 23-6, pl. 253; Cat. Exh. *Flemish Art, 1300-1700*, Royal Academy of Arts, London, 1953-54, p. 62, No. 185; Cat. Exh. Agnew, London, 1961, No. 16.

Prov.: Dr. A.C. von Frey, Paris; Colin Agnew, London; Sir Otto Beit, London. *Sir Alfred Beit, Bt., Russborough, Co. Wicklow, Ireland*

This portrait of Marie de' Medici (1573-1642) was designed as a pendant to that of Anne of Austria, consort of Louis XIII of France. The two paintings are numbered successively in the inventory of Rubens's estate drawn up at his death, and are now both in the Prado, Madrid. Peiresc, in a letter to Rubens dated 14 April 1622, mentions the portraits of the two Queens of France as belonging together. They were painted by Rubens during his first stay in Paris in January-February 1622.

Mother of the King of France and mother-in-law of the King of Spain and the Duke of Savoy, Marie de' Medici was also about to become mother-in-law to the King of England. She was, so to speak, in the very centre of French affairs, and France had suddenly become the pivot of European politics. The rapprochement with Spain and the Catholic peace for which she had striven appeared close at hand. The portrait shows her as a dignified widow, a matriarch at the height of her power, little suspecting that Richelieu's machinations would soon drive her out of France.

Canvas, 130:108 cm.

Bibl.:   *Rooses*, IV, pp. 215, 216, No. 997; *K.d.K.*, p. 268; *Thuillies-Foucart*, pp. 10-29; *Huemer, Portraits I*, No. 27.

Prov.:   Acquired from Rubens's estate by Philip IV of Spain. Transferred from the royal collections to the Prado in 1794.

Museo del Prado, Madrid

The Consignment of the Regency of Maria de' Medici, Musée du Louvre, Paris

In 1622-25 Rubens painted for Marie de' Medici (1573-1642), the Queen Dowager of France, a series of scenes from her life to decorate a wing of the Luxemburg Palace built for the Queen by Salomon de Brosse. The first mention of this project that has survived is in a letter of 1621 to Rubens from Peiresc, who had heard that he was coming to discuss decorations for the Palace. Rubens stayed in Paris during January and February 1622, and signed the contract with Marie de' Medici on 26 February.

As the Queen was on delicate terms with her son Louis XIII, with whom she had just been reconciled, the programme had to be designed with tact so as to avoid over-explicit reference to painful events in the past. Accordingly, in May, Rubens sent a general outline for the Queen's approval. This was accepted with a few modifications, and a year later, in May 1623, Rubens arrived in Paris with nine paintings which he completed there. The rest of the series was delivered in February 1625. The twenty-four allegorical scenes of the Queen's life are now in the Louvre in Paris.

This commission, one of the biggest that Rubens ever received, produced one of the outstanding monuments of baroque art. For several scenes Rubens made more than one sketch, and many of these have survived (see Nos. 63-67).

The Medici cycle (see p. 151) included three portraits, hung at one end of the gallery. Marie de' Medici, represented as Minerva, was in the centre, and to either side were her parents Francesco I de' Medici (1541-87) and Joanna of Austria (1547-78).

Francesco succeeded his father Cosimo I as Grand Duke of Tuscany (Florence and Siena) in 1574. He is depicted in this sketch at full length and in ceremonial costume. His attitude and expression are those of a crafty tyrant. The finished painting (247:116 cm), now in the Louvre in Paris, is certainly not one of the best to have come from Rubens's studio; it follows the sketch in its main lines. See No. 64.

Panel, 32.5:24.5 cm.

Bibl.: *Rooses*, III, p. 254, No. 753[1]; K. Grossmann, *Der Gemäldezyklus der Galerie der Maria von Medici von Peter Paul Rubens*, Strasbourg, 1906, p. 20; *Thuillier-Foucart*, pp. 71, 72.

Prov.: Anonymous sale (directed by Paillet), Paris, 17 February 1774, lot 80; Sané, sold in Paris in 1780; anonymous sales (directed by Le Brun), Paris, 1780 and 1782. Acquired with the Hans West collection in 1809.

Statens Museum for Kunst, Copenhagen

Oil sketch for the Medici cycle (see p. 151). Joanna of Austria, Grand Duchess of Tuscany and mother of Marie de' Medici, is depicted full-length and facing right, so the portrait was presumably hung to the left of that of her daughter. The finished painting (247:116 cm.), now in the Louvre in Paris, follows this sketch in its main lines and, like the portrait of Joanna's spouse Francesco (see No. 63), is certainly not among Rubens's best works.

Panel, 32.5:24.5 cm.

Bibl.: *Rooses*, III, p. 255, No. 754[1]; K. Grossmann, *Der Gemäldezyklus der Galerie der Maria von Medici von Peter Paul Rubens*, Strasbourg, 1906, p. 20; *Thuillier-Foucart*, p. 72.

Prov.: Anonymous sale (directed by Paillet), Paris, 17 February 1774, lot 80; Sané, sold in Paris in 1780; anonymous sales (directed by Le Brun), Paris, 1780 and 1782. Acquired with the Hans West collection in 1809.

Statens Museum for Kunst, Copenhagen

Oil sketch for the Medici cycle (see p. 151). Hymen and Cupid, hovering in mid-air, present Henry IV of France with a portrait of Marie de' Medici, his future consort. The king, encouraged by a figure representing France, contemplates the portrait attentively. At his feet two putti play with his helmet and shield, alluding to the peaceful times that are to follow the marriage. Jupiter and Juno, identified by the eagle and peacock respectively, survey the scene from a cloud and take the royal couple under their protection.

The large finished painting (394:295 cm.), now in the Louvre in Paris, differs very little from the sketch, except for the addition of a spacious landscape in the lower part.

Panel, 48:37 cm.

Bibl.: *Rooses*, III, p. 226, No. 733[1]; K. Grossmann, *Der Gemäldezyklus der Galerie der Maria von Medici von Peter Paul Rubens*, Strasbourg, 1906, pp. 30-3; *Thuillier-Foucart*, pp. 74, 75.

Prov.: Recorded from 1729 in the inventory of the *Residenz*, Munich. Acquired by the Elector Maximilian Emanuel.

Bayerische Staatsgemäldesammlungen, Munich

Oil sketch for the Medici cycle (see p. 151). Henry IV and Marie de' Medici were married by proxy at Florence on 5 October 1600; they did not meet until November 9, as Henry was campaigning against Savoy. According to contemporary records, both spouses were disappointed. Rubens's task was made harder by this fact and by the intimate nature of his theme, but he overcame the difficulty by the use of allegory.

Marie de' Medici and Henry IV, enthroned as Juno and Jupiter and accompanied by Hymen, take each other by the hand as a pledge of wedlock. The Queen, her eyes bashfully cast down, is attended by putti with flambeaux. The city of Lyons, depicted as a young woman with a mural crown on her head, gazes up admiringly; she is seated in a car drawn by two symbolic lions, and the city itself is seen in the background. The lions are led on by Cupid.

The finished painting (394:295 cm.), now in the Louvre in Paris, agrees generally with the present grisaille sketch but differs in some details: Marie de' Medici has no veil, her breast is bare, and Henry IV wears a laurel wreath on his brow.

Panel, 33.5:24.2 cm.

Bibl.: *Rooses*, III, p. 231, No. 726[1]; *Rubens-Bulletijn*, V, pp. 216-20; K. Grossmann, *Der Gemäldezyklus der Galerie der Maria von Medici von Peter Paul Rubens*, Strasbourg, 1906, p. 44; *Evers, 1943*, pp. 299-306; *Thuillier-Foucart*, pp. 77, 78.

Prov.: Abbey of Saint-Ambroise, Paris.

Museum of the Hermitage, Leningrad

This sketch for the Medici cycle (see p. 151) depicts two separate scenes, the apotheosis of Henry IV and the proclamation of his widow as Regent: it was natural to combine these, as the regency was proclaimed four hours after the King's death. On the left Henry, dressed as a Roman general, is raised to heaven by Jupiter and Kronos under the signs of Leo, Virgo and Libra. Other gods, including Hercules and Mercury, look on from Olympus, while Juno gazes at the Queen. Below, Mars's consort Bellona and the naked figure of Victory express their grief at the hero's death in passionate gestures; also the King's murderer flees from the scene, and the Hydra of rebellion is visible. The Queen, dressed in mourning, is enthroned on the right, attended by Minerva (wisdom) and Prudentia (prudence). France, on her knees, offers her a globe ornamented with lilies, signifying royal authority, while Regency, hovering in the air, presents her with the helm of state. The nobles at the foot of the throne demonstrate their loyalty and devotion to the Queen.

In this sketch the groups representing the two themes are too far apart to form a compositional unity, but this is not the case in the final picture (394:727 cm.), now in the Louvre in Paris. In that version the assassin no longer appears, but the Hydra of rebellion is more developed: though scotched, she still raises her head threateningly.

Panel, 53:92 cm.

Bibl.: *Rooses*, III, pp. 238, 239, No. 740[1]; *Thuillier-Foucart*, pp. 82-4.

Prov.: Recorded from 1729 in the inventory of the *Residenz*, Munich. Acquired by the Elector Maximilian Emanuel.

Bayerische Staatsgemäldesammlungen, Munich

The theme of this painting is from the Old Testament (Apocryphal) book of Judith, chapters 8-16. Nebuchadnezzar, king of Assyria, sent his general Holofernes to conquer the Israelites. Holofernes besieged the city of Bethulia, which was on the point of surrendering for want of water. Judith, a beautiful and rich widow, resolved to save the city by seducing Holofernes; she succeeded in beguiling him, and when he was drunk and in a deep sleep she cut of his head and brought it to Bethulia. When the Assyrians learnt that their general was dead, they raised the siege.

In the seventeenth century Judith was regarded as a prefiguration of the Virgin Mary and a symbol of chastity and purity, while Holofernes typified pride and lust.

Judith is seen here, sword in hand, at the moment when she drops the head of Holofernes into a bag held by an old serving-woman. The painting dates from c. 1625; its emphasis is less on the dramatic event than on the beauty of Judith, who wears a dreamy, thoughtful expression. The rapid, skilful execution and the transparent colouring give it a spontaneous, poetic charm.

Rubens made an earlier picture of the same subject, but on that occasion he laid more stress on the ferocity of Judith's act.

Canvas, 113 : 89 cm.

Bibl.: *K.d.K.*, p. 236; R. Oldenbourg, *Zur 'Judith' von Rubens*, in *Zeitschrift für bildende Kunst*, January-February, 1922, pp. 66-8.

Prov.: Contini Bonacossi, Florence; Signora Maria Borghesani, Bologna, sold at Sotheby's, London, 25 June 1924, lot 35; sold to Marshal Hermann Goering in 1942. Loaned by the Italian State.

Soprintendenza per i Beni Artistici e Storici per le Provincie di Firenze e Pistoia, Florence

The Virgin rises through the air, surrounded by angels. On the earth below, in front of a cave, the open coffin is surrounded by holy women and Apostles, including St. John with upraised arms.

A modello for the large altarpiece commissioned by Dean Johannes Del Rio and his heirs for the high altar of Our Lady's church in Antwerp, where it still is. The painting follows the main lines of the sketch, but in it the figures are closer together and nearer the spectator. Although the first negotiations with Del Rio for the altarpiece began in 1618, it was not completed until March 1627, having been delayed by various circumstances including Del Rio's death. The present modello was probably painted *c.* 1625, though some authors are inclined to place it some years earlier. See No. 24.

Panel, 90:61 cm.

Bibl.:   *Burchard*, pp. 2, 3, No. 2; Cat. Exh. *Rotterdam, 1953-54*, p. 71, No. 51; *d'Hulst, 1968*, p. 97, No. 15; C. Van de Velde, *Rubens' hemelvaart van Maria in de Kathedraal te Antwerpen*, in *Jaarboek van het Koninklijk Museum voor Schone Kunsten*, Antwerp, 1975, pp. 270, 271.

Prov.:   John Webb, sold in London, 30-31 May 1821, lot 155, and bought by Davies; F. Thomas Davies, London, 1950; S. and R. Rosenberg, London, 1955. Acquired in 1957.

Koninklijk Kabinet van Schilderijen 'Mauritshuis', The Hague

The Defenders of the Eucharist, Tapestry designed by Rubens. Church of the Señoras
Religiosas Descalzas Reales, Madrid

THE TRIUMPH OF THE EUCHARIST

The *Triumph of the Eucharist* is a sumptuous set of no fewer than twenty tapestries, woven after cartoons executed by Rubens in 1625-27 and commissioned by the Archduchess Isabella Clara Eugenia (1566-1633), daughter of Philip II of Spain and governor of the Southern Netherlands. The series was designed to adorn the convent church of the Señoras Religiosas Descalzas Reales in Madrid, belonging to the discalced Order of the 'Poor Clares': the convent was especially dedicated to worshipping the Eucharist, to which St. Clare of Assisi had a particular devotion. The Infanta Isabella spent eight months there before her mariage, and felt so closely associated with the convent that after her husband, the Archduke Albert, died in 1621 she invariably dressed as a member of the Third Order of 'Poor Clares' on both ecclesiastical and secular occasions. The tapestries, which are still in the convent's possession, were presented by her as a token of devotion and affection. They were woven at Brussels in the studios of Jan Raes and Jacob Geubels and their assistants. Several preliminary sketches and modelli by Rubens are still extant, as well as full-size cartoons on canvas. See Nos. 70-76.

A rough sketch, also known as a bozzetto, for the tapestry cycle *The Triumph of the Eucharist* (see p. 167). The sketch gives an idea of the way in which tapestries were hung in the convent church around and above the high altar on the processional days of Corpus Christi and on Good Friday. The upper register shows two groups of angels making music, while the lower level depicts the leaders of church and state adoring the Sacrament. The significance of the dark area in the middle is uncertain.

Panel, 31.8 : 31.8 cm.

Bibl.:   *Goris-Held*, pp. 34, 35, No. 57; J.S. Held, *Rubens' Triumph of the Eucharist* 1968, 3, pp. 2-22; C. Scribner, *Sacred Architecture: Rubens's Eucharist Tapestries*, in *The Art Bulletin*, LVII, 1975, pp. 519-28, No. 4; Nora De Poorter, *The Eucharist Series, Corpus Rubenianum Ludwig Burchard*, II, Brussels, 1977, Nos. 1-5a.

Prov.: Dowdeswell, Paris, 1914; presented by Mr. and Mrs. Martin A. Ryerson.
        and the Modello in Louisville, in *Bulletin of the J.B. Speed Art Museum*, XXVI,
The Art Institute of Chicago, Mr. and Mrs. Martin A. Ryerson Collection, Chicago, Michigan

Bozzetto for a tapestry in the series *The Triumph of the Eucharist* (see p. 167). Melchizedek, high priest and king of Salem, appearing from behind a Salomonic column on the left, bows to Abraham and offers him bread. Pitchers of wine are seen between them. Melchizedek is attended by two men with a basket of bread; a boy holds the train of his long robe. Abraham is shown as an aged man in armour, accompanied by other warriors. (*Genesis*, 14:18-20). The bread and wine offered by Melchizedek were regarded as a prefiguration of the Holy Sacrament of the Altar.

The whole scene is shown as if on a tapestry hanging from the architrave of the architectonic border. Below is a plinth adorned with angels' heads and festoons.

Panel, 15.6 : 15.6 cm.

Bibl.: *Rooses*, V, p. 307; E. Tormo, *La Apoteosis Eucarística de Rubens: Los tapices de las Descalzas Reales de Madrid*, in *Archivo Español de Arte*, XV, 1942, pp. 22-5, 122; V.H. Elbern, Cat. Exh. *P.P. Rubens, Triumph der Eucharistie*, Essen, 1954-55, pp. 12, 28; Cat. *Fitzwilliam Museum Cambridge*, I, 1960, p. 105, No. 231; Nora De Poorter, *The Eucharist Series, Corpus Rubenianum Ludwig Burchard*, II, Brussels, 1977, No. 7a.

Prov.: Victor Wolfvoet (Antwerp, 1612-52); Samuel Woodburn (London 1786-1853); Thomas Kerrich, whose son, R.E. Kerrich, bequeathed it to the museum in 1873.

The Fitzwilliam Museum, Cambridge

A bozzetto for the largest tapestry in the *Triumph of the Eucharist* series (see p. 167).

Ecclesia, the Church, sits in a triumphal car drawn by four horses. She is a young woman clad in billowing ecclesiastical robes, with a stole over her shoulders and holding up a monstrance. An angel holds the tiara over her head. Two women lead the horses by the bridle, and other angels hover above. An angel mounted on one of the horses carries the *conopeum*, an honorific emblem of the basilical church, with two crossed Papal keys. The car crushes under its wheels Anger, Discord and Hatred; behind it follow Ignorance, with ass's ears, and Blindness, fettered and blindfolded. Below in the centre is a globe wreathed with laurels, symbolizing the Church's rule over the world, and flanked by two lions.

While the allegory is somewhat complicated, its main theme is plain. The dogma of the Eucharist, supported by the Papacy, advances towards final triumph; by this dogma and by its wisdom, the Church will conquer the whole world and rule over it for ever.

Panel, 16.2 : 24.4 cm.

Bibl.: E. Tormo, *La Apoteosis Eucarística de Rubens: Los tapices de las Descalzas Reales de Madrid*, in *Archivo Español de Arte*, XV, 1942, pp. 22-5, 120; V.H. Elbern, Cat. Exh. *P.P. Rubens, Triumph der Eucharistie*, Essen, 1954-55, pp. 12, 37, 38; Cat. *Fitzwilliam Museum Cambridge*, I, 1960, pp. 103, 104, No. 228; Nora De Poorter, *The Eucharist Series, Corpus Rubenianum Ludwig Burchard*, II, Brussels, 1977, No. 11a.

Prov.: Edward Balme?; Thomas Kerrich, whose son, R.E. Kerrich, bequeathed it to the museum in 1873.

The Fitzwilliam Museum, Cambridge

An elaborate modello for the largest tapestry in the *Triumph of the Eucharist* series (see p. 167). It presents in the main, but in reverse direction, the same composition as the bozzetto that preceded it (see No. 72); there are, however, some modifications of detail. In front of the car, for instance, is a woman bearing the labarum, and three women instead of two are leading the horses by the bridle. Small angels are now hovering in front of the monstrance, and others hold up the tapestry on which the whole scene is depicted. The globe below is not encircled by laurels but by a snake biting its tail, the symbol of eternity; instead of lions it is flanked by a rudder (government) and a palm (victory).

Panel, 86 : 105 cm.

Bibl.: *Rooses*, I, pp. 58, 59, No. 43; E. Tormo, *La Apoteosis Eucarística de Rubens: Los tapices de las Descalzas Reales de Madrid*, in *Archivo Español de Arte*, XV, 1942, p. 120; *Van Puyvelde, Esquisses*, p. 81, No. 55, V.H. Elbern, Cat. Exh. *P.P. Rubens, Triumph der Eucharistie*, Essen, 1954-55, pp. 37, 38; Cat. *Museo del Prado*, Madrid, 1975, pp. 292, 293, No. 1698; Nora De Poorter, *The Eucharist Series, Corpus Rubenianum Ludwig Burchard*, II, Brussels, 1977, No. 11b.

Prov.: Royal Spanish collections.

Museo del Prado, Madrid

Bozzetto for a tapestry in the *Triumph of the Eucharist* series (see p. 167).

Seven saints, including the four Latin Fathers of the Church – Ambrose, Augustine, Gregory and Jerome – advance in slow procession. On the left is St. Jerome in a cardinal's hat, and next to him a saint in a biretta, probably St. Norbert. In the centre, St. Thomas Aquinas in a rhetorical attitude, and St. Clare holding a monstrance (in the tapestry she has the features of the Archduchess Isabella). On the right, St. Gregory wearing the papal tiara, St. Augustine with his back to the spectator, and a third indistinct figure who, in the tapestry, can be identified as St. Ambrose. All these were revered as defenders of the Eucharist. The Holy Spirit, in the form of a dove, hovers in the clouds and radiates light over the group. The scene is depicted as if on a tapestry, held up by two cherubs.

Panel, 15.8 : 16.5 cm.

Bibl.: *Rooses*, V, p. 307; E. Tormo, *La Apoteosis Eucarística de Rubens: Los tapices de las Descalzas Reales de Madrid*, in *Archivo Español de Arte*, XV, 1942, pp. 22-5, 130; Cat. *Fitzwilliam Museum Cambridge*, I, 1960, p. 105, No. 241; J.S. Held, *Rubens' Triumph of the Eucharist and the Modello in Louisville*, in *Bulletin of the J.B. Speed Art Museum*, XXVI, 1968, 3, pp. 13, 15, 16; M. Jaffé, *Rediscovered Oil Sketches by Rubens – II*, in *The Burlington Magazine*, CXI, 1969, pp. 537, 538, No. 73; Nora De Poorter, *The Eucharist Series, Corpus Rubenianum Ludwig Burchard*, II, Brussels, 1977, No. 15a.

Prov.: Edward Balme?; Thomas Kerrich, whose son, R.E. Kerrich, bequeathed it to the museum in 1873.

The Fitzwilliam Museum, Cambridge

Bozzetto intended for a tapestry in the *Triumph of the Eucharist* series (see p. 167). The subject was, however, not executed in tapestry form, as Rubens replaced it by *The Meeting of Abraham and Melchizedek* (see No. 71).

In the inventory of the estate of Victor Wolfvoet of Antwerp, who died in 1652, this panel is described as: "A small sketch by Rubens showing angels in a little ship." The ship is setting out at an oblique angle; larger angels, facing the bow, sit at the oars while smaller ones hoist the sail. At the stern is a winged female figure with a bunch of flowering springs in her left hand, while with her right she holds the tiller. At the prow is a large lantern with a candle burning in it. The scene is depicted as if on a tapestry, suspended unsymmetrically in a Tuscan framework.

The design is that of an allegorical 'triumph', with a ship instead of the usual car. The vessel is manned by heavenly beings and guided by the light of Christ (the lantern), as a symbol of the hope inspired in the faithful by the church and the Eucharist.

Panel, 16 : 19 cm.

Bibl.: J.S. Held, *Rubens' Triumph of the Eucharist and the Modello in Louisville*, in *Bulletin of the J.B. Speed Art Museum*, XXVI, 1968, 3, pp. 13, 21, No. 31; J. Müller Hofstede, *Neue Ölskizzen von Rubens*, in *Städel Jahrbuch*, N.F., 2, 1969, pp. 202-5; C. Scribner, *Sacred Architecture: Rubens' Eucharist Tapestries*, in *The Art Bulletin*, LVII, 1975, pp. 524 (No. 18), 525; Nora De Poorter, *The Eucharist Series, Corpus Rubenianum Ludwig Burchard*, II, Brussels, 1977, No. 21.

Prov.: Victor Wolfvoet (Antwerp, 1612-52); Samuel Woodburn (London, 1786-1853); Thomas Kerrich, from 1825; R.E. Kerrich, his son; Albert Hartshorne, grandson of Thomas Kerrich, who bequeathed it in 1910 to Mrs. Wyatt; Oliver E.P. Wyatt, sold at Sotheby's, London, 19 April 1967, lot 13; Dr. A.B. Ashby, London; Dr. Michael Ashby, London, sold at Sotheby's, London, 11 December 1974, lot 29.

Richard L. Feigen & Co., New York

Modello for a tapestry in the *Triumph of the Eucharist* series (see p. 167).

Time, an aged man with wings and a scythe, rises up through the air; in his arms is a young woman personifying Truth, who points to a scroll hanging between clusters of fruit and inscribed: *Hoc est Corpus meum*. Two repellent male figures flee before her. On the left, a heathen altar is overthrown. Luther lies lamenting among his books, Calvin still tries to defend his doctrine, while Tanchelin, another heretic, falls to the ground; he is half-naked and is holding a censer. On the right are two scholars; one, in the background, gazes at the figure of Truth, while the other bows before her and tramples on an apostate monk. Below is a lion with a fox in its claws.

The allegory clearly signifies that, with time, the truth of the Eucharistic dogma will triumph over all the doctrines of its adversaries.

Panel, 86 : 105 cm.

Bibl.: *Rooses*, I, pp. 59, 60, Nos. 44, 44 bis; E. Tormo, *La Apoteosis Eucarística de Rubens: Los Tapices de las Descalzas Reales de Madrid*, in *Archivo Español de Arte*, 1942, pp. 1-26, 117-31, 291-315; *Van Puyvelde, Esquisses*, pp. 31-3; V.H. Elbern, Cat. Exh. *P.P. Rubens, Triumph der Eucharistie*, Essen, 1954-5, p. 33; Cat. *Museo del Prado*, Madrid, 1975, pp. 291, 292 (No. 1697); Nora De Poorter, *The Eucharist Series, Corpus Rubenianum Ludwig Burchard*, II, Brussels, 1977, No. 17b.

Prov.: Royal Spanish collections.

Museo del Prado, Madrid

When David was in the wilderness near Maon he sent messengers to a rich herdsman, Nabal, asking for provisions for his men. Nabal dismissed them empty-handed, whereupon David resolved to avenge himself by the sword. However, Nabal's wife Abigail went to meet David with provisions and so prevented bloodshed. (*I Sam.*, 25: 14-35).

The picture represents Abigail greeting David and showing him the food she has brought. The canvas dates from *c.* 1625-30; a strip has been added at the top by an unknown hand. Another version of this work is in the possession of Dr. G. Henle at Duisburg.

Canvas, 175.2 : 248.9 cm.

Bibl.: *Smith, Catalogue Raisonné*, II, p. 170, No. 592; *Rooses*, I, pp. 147, 148, No. 120; W.R. Valentiner, *Rubens' Paintings in America*, in *The Art Quarterly*, IX, 1946, p. 160, No. 72; *Goris-Held*, p. 32, No. 39; J. Müller Hofstede, *Neue Ölskizzen von Rubens*, in *Städel Jahrbuch*, N.F., II, 1969, p. 239; M. Jaffé, *Rubens' David and Abigail*, in *The Burlington Magazine*, CXIV, 1972, p. 863.

Prov.: Duc de Richelieu; Roger de Piles; duc du Grammont, 1715; Jacques Meijers, sold at Rotterdam, 9 September 1722; Count Plettenberg and Witten, sold at Amsterdam, 2 April 1738; Paul Methuen, London, 1830; M. Secretan, Paris; James E. Scripps, who presented it to the Detroit Institute of Arts, 1889.

The Detroit Institute of Arts, Gift of James E. Scripps, Detroit, Michigan

This painting is notable for the rendering of emotion, particularly the Virgin's reverent love for the Child Jesus and St. Anne's delight in beholding her grandson. From a very early date the work was in the monastery of San Lorenzo at the Escorial, near Madrid, where it hung in the prior's apartments and was much admired. On stylistic grounds it may be dated *c.* 1626-30.

Canvas, 115:90 cm.

Bibl.: P. de los Santos, *Descripción del Real Monasterio de San Lorenzo de El Escorial*, Madrid, 1868, p. 75; *Rooses*, I, pp. 296, 297, No. 222; *Glück*, p. 161; M. Jaffé, *Rediscovered Oil Sketches by Rubens–II*, in *The Burlington Magazine*, CXI, 1969, p. 533; Cat. *Museo del Prado*, 1975, pp. 229-31, No. 1639.

Prov.: Escorial; transferred from there to the Prado in 1839.

Museo del Prado, Madrid

The *Virgin and Child enthroned and surrounded by Saints*, a painting commissioned by the Augustinian monks at Antwerp, was completed by Rubens in 1628 and was immediately placed on the high altar of their church; the subject was a natural one, as the church was dedicated to Our Lady and All Saints.

The present oil sketch is a modello for the painting. The Virgin sits enthroned, while the Child, seated on her lap, places a ring on the finger of St. Catherine; behind the Virgin is St. Joseph and to the right is John the Baptist with an animal's skin over his shoulder. On the left, between the pillars, are Saint Peter and Paul, and at their feet St. Clare of Montefalco and St. Mary Magdalene; in front of these are St. Agnes and St. Apollonia, the latter of whom is invoked against toothache. Below on the left are three soldier saints: St. George with the slain dragon, the naked St. Sebastian and William of Aquitaine, who is seen from behind. Then come three ecclesiastical saints: St. Augustine in episcopal robes, St. Lawrence with the grid on which he was martyred, and St. Nicholas of Tolentino. The holy Family is thus surrounded by fourteen saints, patrons of altars in the church and of the confraternities associated with it.

In the preparation of such a monumental work Rubens left nothing to chance. Far from improvising, he made several preliminary drawings (see No. 159) and oil sketches. Of the compositional sketches that have survived, the present one most closely resembles the final work. See No. 80.

Panel, 79:55 cm.

Bibl.: *Rooses*, I, p. 289, No. 2142; *Van Puyvelde, Esquisses*, p. 82, No. 58; Cat. Exh. *Rotterdam, 1953-54*, p 84, No. 72; P. Bjurström, *Rubens' 'St. George and the Dragon'*, in *The Art Quarterly*, XVIII, 1955, pp. 27-43; F. Grossmann, *Notes on Some Dutch and Flemish Paintings at Rotterdam*, in *The Burlington Magazine*, XCVII, 1955, pp. 335-8; *Baudouin*, pp. 133-7; Cat. *Gemäldegalerie, Staatliche Museen, Berlin*, Berlin-Dahlem, 1975, p. 371, No. 780.

Prov.: Royal Collections, Sanssouci, 1764.

Staatliche Museen Preußischer Kulturbesitz, Gemäldegalerie, Berlin-West

This oil sketch, formerly attributed to Van Dyck, was rightly assigned to Rubens by L. Burchard. It is a detail study for the painting of the *Virgin and Child enthroned and surrounded by Saints*, completed in 1628 and placed on the high altar of the Augustinian church in Antwerp (see under No. 79).

In the sequence of surviving drawings and sketches that preceded the final painting, the present sketch follows on the compositional drawing in Stockholm (see No. 159) and another, looser detail study in oils on panel, also of St. Sebastian and St. George, now in the P. and N. de Boer Foundation, Amsterdam. The two saints appear, in more or less the same attitudes as in the present sketch, in an oil sketch of the whole composition now in the Städelsches Kunstinstitut, Frankfurt-on-Main. However, Rubens was not satisfied with the general effect: his main object was to create a firm counterpoise, in the lower part of the picture, to the impressive form of St. Augustine, while at the same time linking the group of St. Sebastian and St. George closely with the Madonna. He modified this group and added to it the figure of William of Aquitaine, as can be seen from the composition sketch in Berlin (No. 79), which closely resembles the final painting.

Panel, 41 : 30.5 cm.

Bibl.: Cat. Exh. *Rotterdam, 1953-54*, p. 84, under No. 72; P. Bjurström, *Rubens, 'St. George and the Dragon'*, in *The Art Quarterly*, XVIII, 1955, pp. 27-43; F. Grossmann, *Notes on Some Dutch and Flemish Paintings at Rotterdam*, in *The Burlington Magazine*, XCVII, 1955, p. 337.

Prov.: Mancel collection, Caen.

Musée des Beaux-Arts, Caen

A half-length portrait of Philip IV (1605-65) in front of a rich tasselled drapery. He wears sumptuously embroidered court dress with a semi-circular collar *(golilla)*, and with the Order of the Golden Fleece about his neck.

In a letter to the Sieur de Peiresc dated 2 December 1628 Rubens states that since arriving at Madrid as envoy he has executed a portrait of the King on horseback and, at the command of the Archduchess Isabella, has painted heads of all the royal family. A Spanish source also indicates that during his stay at Madrid from September 1628 to April 1629 he painted no less than five portraits of the King; the present work may be one of these. Some critics, however, believe that only the head is entirely Rubens's work.

Canvas, 78.5 : 62.5 cm.

Bibl.:   *Rooses*, IV, pp. 236, 237, No. 1028; *Held*, p. 139, under No. 111; Cat. Exh. *Rubens diplomaat*, Rubens Castle, Elewijt, 1962, pp. 134, 135, No. 67; Enriqueta Harris, *Cassiano dal Pozzo on Diego Velasquez*, in *The Burlington Magazine*, CXII, 1970, pp. 364-73; *Huemer, Portraits I*, No. 35.

Prov.:   Duke of Hamilton, Hamilton Palace, sold at Christie's, London, 17 June 1882, lot 22; Otto Beit, London; Alfred Beit, London. Bought on the art market after 1949 by the Ruzicka Foundation, and loaned by it to the Kunsthaus, Zurich.

Kunsthaus Zürich, Stiftung Prof. Dr. L. Ruzicka, Zurich

Thomas Howard, second Earl of Arundel and Surrey (1585-1646), was made a Knight of the Garter in 1611. He became Earl Marshal of England in 1621, and general of the army sent against Scotland in 1638. In 1642, during the Civil War, he left England for good. His political and military importance are far overshadowed by his role as one of England's first and greatest art connoisseurs and collectors.

This oil sketch is probably a study from life, executed in 1629-30, for the portrait in the Isabella Stewart Gardner Museum in Boston. The Earl, in armour and wearing the ribbon of the Garter, is shown as a man of powerful features, the severity of which is somewhat modified by the expression of his eyes. Another study for the Boston picture, a drawing, is in the Stirling and Francine Clark Art Institute, Williamstown, Mass. (see No. 161).

Canvas, 68,6 : 53.3 cm.

Bibl.: *Smith, Catalogue Raisonné*, II, p. 308, under No. 1128; *Rooses*, IV, p. 128, under No. 890; G. Glück, *Rubens as a Portrait Painter*, in *The Burlington Magazine*, LXXVI, 1940, p. 174; D. Piper, *Catalogue of Seventeenth-Century Portraits in the National Portrait Gallery*, Cambridge, 1963, p. 15, No. 2391.

Prov.: John, fourth Duke of Argyll; his son, Lord Frederick Campbell; William, first Earl of Amherst. Acquired by the National Portrait Gallery in 1929.

National Portrait Gallery, London

One of these two oil sketches shows Justice *(Justitia)* as a young woman holding a sword aloft with one hand and carrying a balance in the other, while trampling on a snake, symbol of evil. Justice protects the virtuous community against the wicked: this is symbolized by the flock of sheep and the fleeing wolf. The second sketch shows Abundance *(Abundantia)* as a young woman with a cornucopia in her lap; Nature's benefits to man, symbolized by the fruit pouring out of it, are gathered up by two putti. The purse under the woman's foot may represent the contrast between material wealth and the profusion of nature. These two sketches were executed *c.* 1630; no larger works after them are known.

Each sketch: panel, 63.7:45.8 cm.

Bibl.: C. Ripa, *Iconologia of uytbeeldingen des Verstands*, Amsterdam, 1644, p. 433; B. Nicolson, *Pictures from Hampshire Houses*, in *The Burlington Magazine*, XCIX, 1957, pp. 273, 274; M. Jaffé, *Unpublished Drawings by Rubens in French Museums*, in *Gazette des Beaux-Arts*, LXVI, 1965, pp. 175-80.

Prov.: In the family of the Earl of Malmesbury, Newnham House, Basingstoke, from the eighteenth century; Victor Thaw, New York.

Artemis, S.A., Brussels

On 16 December 1630, four years after the death of his first wife Isabella Brant, Rubens married the sixteen-year-old Helena Fourment, daughter of an Antwerp merchant. The Cardinal Infante Ferdinand later wrote that she was undoubtedly the most beautiful woman in Flanders (letter to Philip IV of Spain, 27 February 1639). Rubens, in a letter to his friend Peiresc dated 18 December 1634, described his motives as follows: "I took a young wife born of honest but bourgeois parents, although all sought to persuade me to marry a lady of the Court. But I feared to expose myself to pride – a vice often met with in the nobility, especially in that sex – and so I chose one who would not blush when I took up my brushes. And, to tell the truth, I would have been loth to exchange my precious liberty for the embraces of an old woman." The portrait may be dated *c.* 1630-31.

Panel, 96.6 : 69.3 cm.

Bibl.:   *Rooses*, IV, p. 162, No. 937; *K.d.K.*, p. 331; L. Van Puyvelde, *Les portraits des femmes de Rubens*, in *La Revue de l'art ancien et moderne*, LXXI, April 1937, pp. 11-6; *Katalog der Ältere Pinakothek München*, 1936, p. 230, No. 349; H. Vlieghe, *Portraits II*, *Corpus Rubenianum Ludwig Burchard*, XIX (in preparation).

Prov.:   Electoral collection; perhaps acquired in 1698 by the Elector Maximilian Emanuel from the Antwerp merchant Gisbert van Ceulen.

Bayerische Staatsgemäldesammlungen, Munich

The young woman, portrayed full-length and life-size, is seen in front of a landscape; the horizon is low, as the artist's viewpoint is somewhat *di sotto in su*. The background consists of a large grey cloud above which bluish light is breaking through, while below can be seen the glow of the setting sun.

The black satin dress, with a flat collar and lace cuffs and with light violet ribbons, and the broad black hat with a plume, give the subject the dignified appearance of a well-to-do *bourgeoise*. There is an air of innocence about the sitter's elegant attitude and the delicate gesture with which she holds the ostrich plumes she is using as a fan.

This work dates from 1630-32; it is executed broadly but with love and care, and is among Rubens's finest portraits. Some art historians, however, believe that the subject is not Helena but her sister Susanna.

Panel, 187:86 cm.

Bibl.:　*Rooses*, IV, pp. 165, 166, No. 943; K.d.K., p. 329; *Glück*, pp. 118-36; H. Vlieghe, *Portraits II, Corpus Rubenianum Ludwig Burchard*, XIX (in preparation).

Prov.:　Sir Robert Walpole, Earl of Orford, Houghton Hall; Hermitage, Leningrad.

Calouste Gulbenkian Museum, Lisbon

Achilles vanquishing Hector, Tapestry designed by Rubens. Staatliche Kunstsammlungen, Kassel

In 1630 or in the next few years Rubens painted oil sketches for a series of eight tapestries depicting *The History of Achilles*. It is not known who commissioned them, but there is much evidence suggesting that the customer was Daniel Fourment, the Antwerp dealer in silks and tapestries, whose daughter Rubens married on 6 December 1630. Both the sketches and a series of tapestries on *The History of Achilles* figure in the inventory of Fourment's possessions drawn up at his death in 1643. The *editio princeps* was most probably woven by Daniel Eggermans the Elder (died *c*. 1643).

After the sketches larger panels were painted, the modelli, for the double purpose of being shown to prospective buyers of tapestries and of serving as models for the cartoons, which were on the same scale as the tapestries themselves.

For *The History of Achilles*, depicting the life of the Greek hero from infancy to death, Rubens relied chiefly on material to be found in sixteenth-century and contemporary handbooks of mythology. He also used his own knowledge of the classics to depict the various scenes in an antique setting, while emphasizing emotional aspects and especially the power of love. See Nos. 86-88.

Oil sketch for a tapestry in the series *The History of Achilles* (see p. 201).

Thetis, anxious over the fate of her son Achilles, the future hero, dipped him in the waters of the Styx, river of the underworld, in order to make him invulnerable. However, the heel by which she held the baby remained dry, so that this part of him was unprotected: hence the expressions 'Achilles' heel' and 'Achilles tendon'. (Virgil, *Aenaid*, VI, 291, 301-16, 417, 418).

Thetis is shown at the moment when she has half immersed the child. One of the Fates, recognizable by the distaff at her waist, holds a torch to illuminate the scene. In the background Charon in his boat ferries the souls of the dead across the Styx; many are waiting anxiously on the shore. The eeriness of the scene is increased by a bat flitting in the air. The architectural setting includes herms of the underworld deities: Proserpina, with a crescent moon above her forehead, and Pluto with his emblem of a two-pronged fork. These are surmounted by an architrave with, in its centre, a cartouche ornamented with bats' wings and linked to the herms by festoons. Cerberus, the three-headed dog, lies crouching at the base: it is he who admits souls to the underworld and prevents their returning to the land of the living. The figures are shown as left-handed, since they will be reversed in the eventual tapestry. The modello of this piece is in the John and Mable Ringling Museum of Art at Sarasota, Florida.

Panel, 43 : 36.5 cm.

Bibl.: *Smith, Catalogue Raisonné*, II, No. 849; *Van Puyvelde, Esquisses*, pp. 40, 41, 94, 95; *Burchard*, pp. 13-5; Cat. Exh. *Rotterdam, 1953-54*, No. 61; *d'Hulst, 1968*, pp. 100, 101, No. 20; *Haverkamp Begemann*, pp. 95, 96, No. 1a.

Prov.: Daniel Fourment, Antwerp, to 1643; Jean-Henry Gobelinus, Brussels, to 1681; Joan Baptista Anthoine, Antwerp, to 1691; Richard Mead, to 1754; Fulk Greville, to 1794; John Smith-Barry, Marbury Hall, Northwich, Cheshire, c. 1814; A.H. Smith-Barry; Lord Barrymore, sold at Sotheby's, London, 21 June 1933, lot 28; Goudstikker, Amsterdam. Presented to the museum in 1933 by D.G. van Beuningen.

Boymans-van Beuningen Museum, Rotterdam

Modello for a tapestry in the series *The History of Achilles* (see p. 201).

Achilles, having quarrelled with Agamemnon, refused to take further part in the siege of Troy, but lent his armour to his friend Patroclus. The latter, however, was killed in battle by Hector and, the armour thus being lost, Thetis requested Hephaestus, the god of fire and the smithy, to make a new set for Achilles (Homer, *Iliad*, XVIII).

Thetis, rising from the sea, receives a shield from Hephaestus's hands, aided by the latter's wife Charis and by a putto. One of the god's assistants brings forward a cuirass, while another putto presents a helmet to a triton. Two assistants are seen in the background in the ruddy glow of the smithy. The scene is enclosed in an architectural framework with two herms, personifying Juno with her peacock and Jupiter with the eagle and thunderbolt. Above, on the architrave, is a cartouche with festoons supported by putti on either side; at the base are Hephaestus's tools and an anvil on which something is burning.

Panel, 108.5 : 126 cm.

Bibl.:   *Rooses*, III, p. 40; *Van Puyvelde, Esquisses*, pp. 36-8, 87, 88; *Burchard*, pp. 15, 16, No. 13; [A. Seilern], *Flemish Paintings and Drawings at 56, Princes Gate, London*, London, 1955, pp. 58, 59; Cat. Exh. *Rotterdam, 1953-54*, pp. 81, 82, No. 66; *d'Hulst, 1968*, p. 102, under No. 24; *Haverkamp Begemann*, pp. 115, 116, No. 4c.

Prov.:   Daniel Fourment, Antwerp?; Peter Fourment, Antwerp, to 1653; Gerard van der Strecken, Jan van Leefdael, Hendrick Lenaerts, Brussels; duque de Infantado, Madrid, to 1841; duque de Pastrana, Madrid. Presented to the museum in 1887.

Musée des Beaux-Arts, Pau

Modello for a tapestry in the series *The History of Achilles* (see p. 201).

The Trojans withdrew within the walls of their city, leaving Hector to engage in single combat with Achilles (Homer, *Iliad*, XXII).

Hector, wearing the armour stripped from Patroclus, is forced on to one knee by Achilles; the latter, wearing the splendid armour forged by Hephaestus, drives his spear through Hector's throat. Athene (Minerva), enveloped in a cloud, hovers above and protects the conqueror. The despairing Trojans are seen in the background. The scene is depicted in an architectural setting with two herms personifying Hercules and Mars: the former with the lion's skin on his shoulders, his club resting against the base of the herm; the latter wearing a helmet, with a sword under his belt and other weapons against the base. Above, on the architrave, is a cartouche with festoons on either side; two putti, supporting these, look down anxiously at the heroes' duel. At the base are two fighting cocks.

This modello is based on an oil sketch in the Boymans-van Beuningen Museum at Rotterdam, which, however, shows instead of the fighting cocks a plinth with a cornucopia on either side.

Panel, 108.5 : 125 cm.

Bibl.: *Rooses*, III, p. 40; *Van Puyvelde, Esquisses*, pp. 36-8, 87, 88; *Burchard*, pp. 15, 16; Cat. Exh. *Rotterdam, 1953-54*, pp. 72-82; *d'Hulst, 1968*, p. 103, under No. 25; *Haverkamp Begemann*, pp. 133, 134, No. 7b.

Prov.: Duque de Infantado, Madrid, to 1841; duque de Pastrana, Madrid. Presented to the museum in 1887.

Musée des Beaux-Arts, Pau

Rubens painted the theme of the Holy Family several times. Apart from the Virgin and Child, considerable variation was possible as regards the décor and choice of figures. In this version the attention is centred on the Child asleep on Mary's lap; the Virgin, St. Joseph and St. Anne regard him with profound affection. The free handling and bright colours point to a late date of execution, *c.* 1630-35. Several copies of this painting were made in the studio.

Canvas, 174 : 142 cm.

Bibl.:   W.R. Valentiner, *Rubens' Paintings in America*, in *The Art Quarterly*, IX, 1946, pp. 153-68; Cat. *North Carolina Museum of Art*, Raleigh, 1956, p. 65, No. 129.

Prov.:   Captain Askew-Robertson, Ladykirk, Norham-on-Tweed, Scotland.

The North Carolina Museum of Art, Raleigh, North Carolina

Ildefonso, a seventh-century Benedictine and Archbishop of Toledo, was a zealous champion of the Immaculate Conception. Legend relates that, during a noctural procession in the cathedral, he had a vision of the Virgin seated on the bishop's throne; surrounded by a company of female saints, she presented Ildefonso with a chasuble as a sign of gratitude. This oil sketch depicts the scene and, to either side, the Archdukes Albert and Isabella as donors, with their respective patron saints.

The sketch is a study for the large triptych of c. 1630-32, presented by Isabella to the church of Saint-Jacques-sur-le-Coudenberg in Brussels to adorn the altar in the chapel of the confraternity of St. Ildefonso. In the triptych itself, now in the Kunsthistorisches Museum at Vienna, the donors are depicted separately on the side panels.

Canvas, 53 : 83 cm.

Bibl.: *Rooses*, II, pp. 306-8, No. 456bis; *Held*, p. 139; G. Aust, *Entwurf und Ausführung bei Rubens*, in *Wallraf-Richartz Jahrbuch*, XX, 1958, p. 188; *Burchard-d'Hulst, 1963*, pp. 289-91; *Martin, Ceiling Paintings*, pp. 183, 184; *Vlieghe, Saints*, II, pp. 86-8, No. 117b.

Prov.: Clemens August, Duke of Bavaria, Elector and Archbishop of Cologne; Boileau, Paris?; Count Karl Cobenzl (Vienna, Brussels, 1712-70)?. Acquired by Catharine II of Russia, probably in 1768.

Museum of the Hermitage, Leningrad

Rubens's painting of the Garden of Love is akin to the traditional Netherlands theme of a garden showing people enjoying life. The content, however, cannot be fully grasped without some explanation of its allegorical meaning.

Four human couples, two on either side, surround a central group of three young women representing the Graces, who bestow on mankind the blessing of festive meetings. Their temple is seen in the background, and in it they are represented again in the form of an antique sculptural group. Also in the background is a separate group of young people engaged in a round game. Above right, as a sculptured figure on a fountain, the love-goddess Venus Victrix dominates the scene. The warm nourishment flows from her breast, while two putti leap forth and carry her message to mankind. Another putto, hovering in the centre of the scene, illuminates the sculptured Graces with a torch and holds a crown over the heads of the Graces represented by three young women. Above left, two or three more putti approach swiftly; the foremost one is, as it were, drawn along by a pair of doves, symbolizing conjugal love, and holds a yoke in his hand, signifying wedlock.

This magnificent painting was executed by Rubens c. 1632-33. Another version is at Wadesdon Manor, Buckinghamshire, England. Christoffel Jegher made a woodcut of the subject after a drawn model by Rubens. See Nos. 164-166.

Canvas, 198 : 283 cm.

Bibl.: *Rooses*, IV, pp. 63-7, No. 835; G. Glück, *Rubens' Liebesgarten*, in *Jahrbuch der Kunsthistorischen Sammlungen*, XXXV, Vienna, 1920, pp. 49-98; L. Burchard, in *Glück*, pp. 383-9; *Evers, 1942*, p. 339 e.a.; *Burchard-d'Hulst, 1956*, pp. 104, 105, under No. 128; *Held*, pp. 153, 154, under No. 152; W. Burchard, *The 'Garden of Love' by Rubens*, in *The Burlington Magazine*, CV, 1963, pp. 428-32; *Burchard-d'Hulst, 1963*, pp. 278-81, under No. 180; A. Süberkrüb, *Der Liebesgarten*, Bern-Frankfurt a.d. M., 1975; Cat. *Museo del Prado*, Madrid, 1975, pp. 230-32, No. 1690.

Prov.: Recorded from 1666 in the Royal Spanish collections.

Museo del Prado, Madrid

This evening scene with a cart on a sunken path is typical of Rubens's later landscapes, though he used the cart motif in earlier works as well. The warm colours, the rich play of light and shade and the rhythmic movement of the trees combine to render admirably the atmosphere of a quiet evening, while at the same time evoking the deeper forces and vitality of exuberant nature. See No. 42.

Panel, 49.5 : 54.7 cm.

Bibl.: *Rooses*, IV, p. 393, No. 1205; *K.d.K.*, p. 271; G. Glück, *Die Landschaften von Peter Paul Rubens*, Vienna, 1945, p. 67, No. 32; D. Hannema, *Catalogue of the D.G. von Beuningen Collection*, Rotterdam, 1949, p. 69, No. 59; Cat. Exh. *Rotterdam, 1953-54*, pp. 100, 101, No. 94; Cat. Exh. *Brussels, 1965*, p. 201, No. 211.

Prov.: Marquis of Camden, sold in London, 12 June 1841; Samuel Rogers, sold in London, 3 May 1856; Thomas Baring, London; Earl of Northbrook, Micheldever, Stratton, Hampshire; F. Koenings, Haarlem; D.G. van Beuningen, Vierhouten. Acquired with the D.G. van Beuningen collection in 1958.

Boymans-van Beuningen Museum, Rotterdam

The Apotheosis of James I, Banqueting House, London

CEILING DECORATION OF THE BANQUETING HOUSE, LONDON

A letter of 13 September 1621 from Rubens to William Trumbull already speaks of decorating "the hall in the new palace", but for eight years the documents make no further mention of the project. Rubens probably received the definitive commission from Charles I during his stay in London in 1629-30. This involved nine large allegorical ceiling decorations for the Banqueting House in Whitehall, completed by Inigo Jones in 1622. The ceiling paintings are still to be seen there, and are the only work of this kind by Rubens that has survived. Their theme is the glorification of the reign of Charles's father James I. It is known from Rubens's correspondence with Balthazar Gerbier that the series was nearly completed by 11 August 1634 and that the paintings reached England in November or December of the following year.

The series comprises an oval piece in the centre of the ceiling, adjoined by two square and two rectangular ones, with four smaller oval paintings in the corners. The general arrangement, and also various details, are based on Venetian models, especially Veronese's ceilings in the Doges' Palace; those of Giulio Romano at Mantua also seem to have influenced Rubens's design.

Many sketches for the ceiling decoration have survived, either of the whole composition or of separate parts (see No. 93).

An oil sketch for the left-hand half of one of the large ceiling paintings in the Banqueting House, Whitehall, London (see p. 217), entitled *The Union of England and Scotland*. The two kingdoms were united in the person of James VI of Scotland, who became James I of England on 24 March 1603. The Prince of Wales, afterwards Charles I, was born on 19 November 1600 and was thus two and a half years old.

Two female figures, personifying England and Scotland, place a double crown on the head of the young prince (or possibly the infant realm of Great Britain). The helmeted figure of Minerva, or Britannia, brings the two crowns together. Above, two hovering putti support the escutcheon of the United Kingdom; below, a putto with a torch sets fire to implements of war, indicating that all quarrels between England and Scotland are now at an end.

A composition sketch for the whole ceiling painting is in the Hermitage at Leningrad; an earlier and somewhat smaller version of the present sketch belongs to the Boymans-van Beuningen Museum at Rotterdam. Another sketch, in the City Art Gallery, Birmingham (collection of Lieutenant-Colonel H.R. Davies), shows only the enthroned James I with some accompanying figures.

Panel, 83 : 71 cm.

Bibl.: *Smith, Catalogue Raisonné*, II, pp. 232, 233, No. 814; *Rooses*, III, pp. 286, 287, No. 769; *The Minneapolis Institute of Arts Bulletin*, XV, 1926, pp. 154-6, No. 29; *Van Puyvelde, Esquisses*, pp. 86, 87, No. 72; *Goris-Held*, p. 40, No. 86; Cat. Exh. *Rotterdam, 1953-54*, p. 95, No. 86; O. Millar, *Rubens: The Whitehall Ceiling*, London, 1958; J.S. Held, *Rubens's Glynde Sketch and the Installation of the Whitehall Ceiling*, in *The Burlington Magazine*, CXII, 1970, pp. 274-81.

Prov.: King Charles I of England; Sir Joshua Reynolds (London, 1723-92); Prince Demidoff of San Donato, 1888; Charles Porgès, Paris; C. Sedelmeyer, Paris; A. Lehmann, Paris.

The Minneapolis Institute of Arts, The William Hood Dunwoody Fund, Minneapolis

Ferdinand, the third son of Philip III of Spain, was born on 16 May 1609. He was made a cardinal in 1619, at the age of ten, and in the following year Archbishop of Toledo, though he was never ordained. He became chiefly noted as a brilliant commander.

In 1631 it was announced that he was being sent to help his aunt Isabella, who was advancing in years and had been a widow since 1621, to govern the Southern Netherlands. However, he did not arrive there for another two or three years. In 1633 he set sail from Barcelona for Genoa, but the further journey was interrupted several times. In 1634 he joined the Imperial army at Nördlingen in Bavaria, where on 6 September the Spanish and Austrian troops heavily defeated the Swedes. On 17 April 1635 he at last made his solemn entry into the city of Antwerp, which was richly decorated for the occasion under Rubens's direction. (See also Nos. 95, 96). Two full-length portraits of him by Rubens figured on triumphal arches.

Canvas, 125 : 90 cm.

Bibl.: *K.d.K.*, p. 376; L. Burchard, Cat. Exh. *Loan Exhibition of Rubens,* Wildenstein, New York, 1951, p. 53, No. 31; *Martin, Pompa Introitus,* pp. 152, 153, under No. 39.

Prov.: Sir Joshua Reynolds (London, 1723-92); Earl of Upper Ossory; Lord Lyviden; Vernon Smith; J. Pierpont Morgan, Dover House, London, 1898.

The John and Mable Ringling Museum of Art, Sarasota, Florida

On 17 April 1635 the Cardinal Infante Ferdinand of Spain, the new governor-general of the Netherlands, made a brilliant ceremonial entry into the city of Antwerp, which was festively decorated for the occasion under Rubens's direction (see under No. 94).

This modello was a design for the rear face of the Arch of Ferdinand, one of the triumphal arches erected on that occasion, in the Lange Nieuwstraat opposite the Markgravestraat. The arch celebrated the Cardinal Infante's victory at Nördlingen on 6 September 1634, when he and his cousin Ferdinand of Hungary, at the head of a Spanish-Austrian army, inflicted a crushing defeat on the Swedes. The battle was depicted on the front of the arch, while, as this sketch shows, the rear face commemorated the victory in the form of an antique triumph; it was also decorated with portraits of the Cardinal Infante and his cousin and with various allegorical figures.

The Triumph of Ferdinand, which originally adorned the rear face of the arch, was painted after Rubens's modello by Jan van den Hoecke and later restored by Jordaens; it is now in the Uffizi at Florence.

Panel, transferred to canvas, 104:72.5 cm.

Bibl.: *Rooses*, III, p. 313; Irmengard von Rader-Baumbach, *Versieringen bij Blijde Inkomsten gebruikt in de Zuidelijke Nederlanden gedurende de 16e en 17e eeuw*, Antwerp-Utrecht, 1943, pp. 65, 66; *Van Puyvelde, Esquisses*, p. 39; *Martin, Pompa Introitus*, pp. 156-8, No. 40a.

Prov.: Prosper Hendrik Lankrink (London, 1628-92), sold in London, 23 January 1693; Robert Walpole, first Earl of Orford (Houghton Hall, 1676-1745); sold in 1779 by George Walpole, third Earl of Orford (1730-91) to Catherine II of Russia.

Museum of the Hermitage, Leningrad

Oil sketch for a triumphal arch erected on the occasion of the state entry of the Cardinal Infante Ferdinand of Spain into Antwerp on 17 April 1635 (see under No. 94). This arch was in the Kloosterstraat in front of St. Michael's Abbey (which no longer exists) and marked the terminal point of the procession. Including the ornamentation at the top it was over 15 metres high, and its breadth was nearly 10 metres.

From the iconographical point of view this arch belongs to the group of decorations designed to honour Ferdinand, but it differs from the others in being purely allegorical and not historical. The principal element of the front face is a painting of *Hercules at the Crossroads*: Ferdinand, in the guise of Hercules, is shown resisting the temptations of Venus and Bacchus and, under Minerva's inspiration, resolving to practise the military virtues.

The architectural parts of the sketch are much less finished than the figurative sections; in some places the preliminary drawing of the architecture in black chalk is still visible.

Panel transferred to canvas, 103 : 72 cm.

Bibl.:   *Rooses*, III, p. 323; E. Panofsky, *Hercules am Scheidewege*, Berlin, 1930, p. 121; K.d.K., p. 367; *Van Puyvelde, Esquisses*, p. 39; *Martin, Pompa Introitus*, pp. 208, 209, No. 52a.

Prov.:   Prosper Hendrik Lankrink (London, 1628-92), sold in London, 23 January 1693; Robert Walpole, first Earl of Orford (Houghton Hall, 1676-1745); sold in 1779 by George Walpole, third Earl of Orford (1730-91) to Catherine II of Russia.

Museum of the Hermitage, Leningrad

Rubens painted more than one altarpiece of the Assumption, and made several preliminary studies for each. The present work is a modello for an altarpiece of *c.* 1635, originally in the Carthusian church at Brussels and now in the Liechtenstein collection at Vaduz. Two modelli have survived: the other is an oil sketch in the collection of Count A. Seilern in London, rich in colour and highly finished. The present painting from Yale is less colourful and more summarily executed. E. Haverkamp Begemann regards it as a second step towards the final altarpiece, showing how Rubens concentrated on the figure of the Virgin and especially the triumphant gesture of her right arm. Her pose, too, is more frontal and is close to that seen in the final painting.

Panel, 56 : 40.5 cm.

Bibl.:   *Smith, Catalogue Raisonné*, II, p. 53, No. 149; *Rooses*, II, p. 184, under No. 360; E. Haverkamp Begemann, '*The Assumption of the Virgin*' – *a hitherto unknown 'modello' by Rubens*, in *The Burlington Magazine*, CIX, 1967, pp. 705, 706.

Prov.:   P. Panné, sold at Christie's, London, on 27 March 1819, lot 109?; Peter Ranier; purchased at the beginning of this century by Walter Lippincott Goodwin, Hartford, father of Henry Sage Goodwin, who presented it to the Yale University Art Gallery in 1965.

Yale University Art Gallery, Gift of Henry Sage Goodwin, New Haven, Connecticut

This painting depicts the dramatic moment of Christ's fall on the road to Calvary. The uphill procession is headed by haughty soldiers with banners; behind Christ the two thieves are dragged to the place of execution. Amid the turmoil are the sorrowful Virgin and St. John, and the wailing daughters of Jerusalem with their offspring. Veronica compassionately wipes the forehead of Christ, while Simon of Cyrene, helped by another man, lifts up the heavy cross. Christ raises himself painfully on his left hand and looks, as it were, towards the spectator.

This work, highly finished and rich in colour, was a modello for the altarpiece formerly in the Benedictine abbey at Affligem and now in the Brussels museum. Rubens received the commission in 1634, and the altarpiece was placed in the church on 8 April 1637. The composition underwent several modifications between this modello and the final painting, owing *inter alia* to the oblong shape of the altar portico, rounded at the top.

Panel, 74:55 cm.

Bibl.: *Rooses*, II, pp. 66, 67, No. 274bis; J. Zarnowski, *Une esquisse nouvellement trouvée de la Montée au Calvaire de Rubens*, in *Jaarboek der Koninklijke Museums voor Schone Kunsten van België*, I, 1938, pp. 163-9, 179; *Van Puyvelde, Esquisses*, pp. 18, 19, 47, 88, Nos. 79-81; Cat. Exh. *Rotterdam, 1953-54*, pp. 98-100, No. 92; E. Haverkamp Begemann, *Rubens' Schetsen*, in *Bulletin Museum Boymans*, V, 1954, p. 8; J. Bruyn, *Rubens' Schets voor de Kruisdraging*, in *Bulletin Rijksmuseum*, 1959, pp. 3-9; *d'Hulst, 1968*, p. 108, No. 36; P.J.J. Van Thiel, C.J. De Bruyn Kops, Jola Cleveringa, W. Kloek, Annemarie Vels Heyn, *All the paintings of the Rijksmuseum in Amsterdam. A completely illustrated catalogue*, Amsterdam-Maarssen, 1976, pp. 485, 489, No. A344.

Prov.: Jacques Meyers, sold at Rotterdam, 9 September 1722, lot 76; Van Heeteren, from whose collection it was acquired in 1809.

Rijksmuseum, Amsterdam

St. Francis bows humbly and reverently before the Child on its mother's lap; St. Joseph and St. Elizabeth look on, while the infant St. John plays with the Child. The free, flowing style of the painting points to a date in the 1630s and indicates that Rubens had at least a considerable hand in it.

Variants of the work are in the Royal collection at Windsor and the San Diego museum, California. The order in which the three versions were painted is a matter of dispute.

Canvas, 175.5 : 201.5 cm.

Bibl.:   *Smith, Catalogue Raisonné*, II, p. 221, under No. 784; *Rooses*, I, p. 309, No. 235; *Glück,* pp. 166 (No. 380), 395; *Goris-Held*, pp. 33 (No. 48), 50 (under No. A48); L. Burchard, Cat. Exh. *Loan Exhibition of Rubens*, Wildenstein, New York, 1951, p. 21, No. 21.

Prov.:   J.P. Miles, Leigh Court, Bristol, 1822; Sir Philip Miles, sold at Christie's, London, 28 June 1884, lot 61; Sir Cecily Miles, sold at Christie's, London, 13 May 1899, lot 26; James Henry Smith, who presented it to the museum in 1902.

The Metropolitan Museum of Art, Gift of James Henry Smith, New York

The amorous relations of Mars and Venus were a popular theme of seventeenth-century painting. In this scene Venus, seated on a couch, presses her breast so that milk spurts into the mouth of the young Cupid, who is climbing on to her lap. Mars, the god of war, sits somewhat apart from them, while a putto on a table beside him loosens the clasps of his armour. It is not clear whether Mars is departing or returning.

Rubens may have intended the mythological figures in this picture to be interpreted allegorically, representing the Christian virtues of Charity and Fortitude. The painting may be dated to the second half of the 1630s.

Canvas, 192.8 : 130.6 cm.

Bibl.: *Smith, Catalogue Raisonné*, II, pp. 196, 197, No. 704; *Rooses*, III, p. 188, 189, No. 704; *K.d.K.*, p. 330; Cat. Exh. *Flemish Art, 1300-1700*, Royal Academy of Arts, London, 1953-54, p. 60, No. 177.

Prov.: Philippe, duc d'Orléans (d. 1723); Benjamin Vandergucht sale, Christie's, London, 11 March 1796, lot 42; Bryan sale, London, 19 May 1798, lot 19; sold at Amsterdam, 27 April 1803. Presented by Bourgeois in 1811.

The Governors of Dulwich College, Picture Gallery, London

Jupiter, surprised by Juno with his beloved Io, turned her into a white heifer; but Juno saw through the deceit, captured the heifer and set Argus to guard her. Jupiter, unable to bear the sight of Io's suffering, rescued her with the aid of Mercury, who lulled Argus into a deep sleep by playing the flute and then cut his head off.

The story is taken from the painters' secular bible, Ovid's *Metamorphoses* (I, 568-721). The painting shows Mercury about to draw his sword and slay the sleeping Argus, while Juno looks on from the clouds. On stylistic grounds this fine painting can be dated *c.* 1635-38. Rubens himself extended it at the top and on both sides.

Panel, 63 : 87.5 cm.

Bibl.:   *Smith, Catalogue Raisonné*, II, p. 85; *Rooses*, III, pp. 122, 123, No. 644; *Oldenbourg*, p. 410.

Prov.:   Purchased in 1742 by de Brais in Paris for Augustus II of Saxony (III of Poland) (1733-63).

Staatliche Kunstsammlungen, Gemäldegalerie Alte Meister, Dresden, DDR

Mercury and Argus. Museo del Prado, Madrid

THE DECORATION OF THE TORRE DE LA PARADA

At the end of 1636 Philip IV of Spain commissioned from Rubens a set of paintings to adorn the newly built hunting lodge, the Torre de la Parada, in the forest of El Pardo, about ten miles from Madrid.

We are fairly well informed as to the history of the series thanks to the correspondence between the King and his brother the Cardinal Infante Ferdinand, who was Governor-General of the Southern Netherlands from 1635 and acted as intermediary. There were originally over sixty paintings of mythological subjects, mostly from Ovid's *Metamorphoses*. Rubens furnished the preparatory sketches, while the actual paintings were done by himself or by assistants such as Cornelis de Vos, Jan Cossiers, Jacob Jordaens, Erasmus Quellinus and Theodoor van Thulden. In addition Rubens was responsible for having fifty hunting scenes and animal studies executed by specialists. The paintings of animals were mostly done by Paul de Vos, while Pieter Snayers undertook some landscapes with a staffage of hunting scenes. The entire decoration of the Torre was completed by the beginning of 1638.

Owing to vandalism and neglect, especially in the eighteenth century, several works were destroyed or dispersed, but about fifty of Rubens's sketches and forty of the final paintings are still extant. See Nos. 102-105.

Oil sketch for the decoration of the Torre de la Parada near Madrid (see p. 237). The subject is taken from a story in the *Onomasticon* of the second-century Roman sophist Julius Pollux, who relates that Hercules' dog once bit a snail (the murex) which stained its muzzle purple: this was the first discovery of the dye for which Tyre became famous.

Theodoor van Thulden's painting after this sketch is in the Prado at Madrid.

Panel, 28 : 34 cm.

Bibl.:   M. Jaffé, *Esquisses inédites de Rubens pour la Torre de la Parada*, in *La Revue du Louvre et des Musées de France*, 1964, p. 316; *Alpers*, pp. 221, 222, No. 31a.

Prov.:   Duque de Infantado; General Victor-Bernard Derrecagaix (Bayonne, 1833-1915). Presented to the city of Bayonne by Mme. Derrecagaix in 1921.

Musée Bonnat, Bayonne

This oil sketch for the decoration of the Torre de la Parada near Madrid (see p. 237) shows an incident in the tale of Cupid and Psyche (Apuleius, *Metamorphoses*, V, 22).

Psyche, curious as to the mysterious lover husband who only visited her by night, lit a lamp and discovered that it was Cupid himself; she is here seen gazing at him admiringly. The painting after this sketch was executed by an unknown assistant of Rubens's; only a fragment of it survives, and is now in the Prado at Madrid.

Psyche's attitude strongly resembles that of the same figure in an early painting of the subject dated *c.* 1612-15, in the collection of Prof. Dr. Rolf Stödter at Hamburg. The composition and the nocturnal setting reflect Rubens's interest in the famous example of Giulio Romano, who painted *Cupid and Psyche* on the ceiling of the Sala di Psiche in the Palazzo del Tè at Mantua.

Panel, 26:25 cm.

Bibl.: M. Jaffé, *Esquisses inédites de Rubens pour la Torre de la Parada*, in *La Revue du Louvre et des Musées de France*, 1964, pp. 314, 315, 318; *Alpers*, p. 196, No. 13a.

Prov.: Duque de Infantado; General Victor-Bernard Derrecagaix (Bayonne, 1833-1915). Presented to the city of Bayonne by Mme. Derrecagaix in 1921.

Musée Bonnat, Bayonne

Oil sketch for the decoration of the Torre de la Parada, a royal hunting lodge near Madrid (see p. 237).

The subject, from Ovid's *Metamorphoses* (I, 689-712), is that of the nymph Syrinx being turned into a reed as she is about to be seized by Pan, god of the woods, who is shown as a half-human, half-animal figure. The painting after the sketch is lost; according to the inventory of the Torre de la Parada in 1794 it was by Erasmus Quellinus.

Panel, 27.8 : 27.8 cm.

Bibl.: M. Jaffé, *Esquisses inédites de Rubens pour la Torre de la Parada*, in *La Revue du Louvre et des Musées de France*, 1964, p. 316; *Alpers*, pp. 247, 248, No. 47a.

Prov.: Duque de Infantado; General Victor-Bernard Derrecagaix (Bayonne, 1833-1915). Presented by Mme. Derrecagaix to the city of Bayonne in 1921.

Musée Bonnat, Bayonne

One of the large paintings executed by Rubens himself to decorate the Torre de la Parada near Madrid (see p. 237).

The scene depicts Eurytus, one of the Centaurs invited to the marriage of Hippodamia to Pirithous, king of the giant Lapiths, in the act of trying to carry off the bride. She was rescued by the hero Theseus after a fearful battle that ended with the defeat of the Centaurs (Ovid, *Metamorphoses*, XII, 210-338).

The preliminary oil sketch for this painting is in the Brussels museum.

Canvas, 182 : 290 cm.

Bibl.:   *Smith, Catalogue Raisonné*, II, p. 138, No. 493; *Rooses*, III, pp. 24, 25, No.
         539; *Alpers*, pp. 229, 230, No. 37.

Prov.:   Torre de la Parada; Royal Palace, Madrid.

Museo del Prado, Madrid

This is sometimes regarded as a portrait of Susanna Fourment (1599-1643), an elder sister of Helena, Rubens's second wife. Susanna married Raymond del Monte in 1617 and then, in 1622, Arnold Lunden. It is far from certain, however, that the portrait is actually of her.

Some alterations in the painting appear to be by another hand: e.g. the hat originally had a broader brim, but has been turned into a 'Spanish' hat. The hands, too, are weak and can scarcely be by Rubens. All this suggests that he left the portrait unfinished and that it was subsequently completed by another artist. The original part probably dates from c. 1636-38.

Panel, 78.2 : 58.7 cm.

Bibl.:   G.F. Waagen, *Die Gemäldesammlung in der Kaiserlichen Eremitage zu St. Peters-burg*, St. Petersburg, 1870, p. 403; W.R. Valentiner, *Rubens' Paintings in America*, in *The Art Quarterly*, IX, 1946, 2, p. 168, No. 140; *Goris-Held*, pp. 26, 27, No. 5; Otto Benesch, Review of *Goris-Held*, in *Kunstchronik*, VII, 1954, p. 76; D. Hannema, *Beschrijvende catalogus Stichting Willem van der Vorm*, Rotterdam, 1962, p. 49, No. 70; H. Vlieghe, *Portraits II, Corpus Rubenianum Ludwig Burchard*, XIX (in preparation).

Prov.:   Probably in the possession of descendants of the Lunden family, c. 1770; Count Stroganoff, St. Petersburg, 1793; Hermitage, Leningrad; David Bing-ham, New York.

Willem van der Vorm Foundation, Rotterdam

By a will dated 24 April 1639 Jan van Vucht, Balthasar Moretus's agent in Madrid, bequeathed this painting *"de la mano del famoso maestro P⁰ Pablo Rubens"* to the Royal Hospital of San Andrés de los Flamencos, a charitable institution for Flemings in Madrid. The work was probably painted shortly before, in 1638 or the beginning of 1639. The composition, with the Saint tied hand and foot to the 'St. Andrew's cross', derives from a picture of the same subject painted between 1594 and 1599 by Rubens's teacher Otto van Veen, which then adorned the church of St. Andrew in Antwerp. The mounted soldier, the kneeling woman and the two figures in the distance are reminiscent of Rubens's *Coup de lance* in the Antwerp museum.

Canvas, 307:217 cm.

Bibl.: A. Palomino, *El Museo Pictórico*, III, Madrid, 1724, p. 298; N. Caïmo, *Voyage d'Espagne, fait en l'année 1755*, II, Paris, 1772, p. 133; *Smith, Catalogue Raisonné*, II, p. 130; *Rooses*, II, pp. 216-8; M. Rooses, *De schenker der Martelie van den H. Andreas aan het gasthuis der Vlamingen te Madrid*, in *Rubens-Bulletijn*, V, 1900, pp. 121-37; *Vlieghe, Saints*, I, pp. 87-9, No. 62.

Prov.: The picture has always been in the chapel of the Royal Hospital of San Andrés de los Flamencos.

Property of the Real Diputación de S. Andrés de los Flamencos, Chapel of S. Andrés de los Flamencos, Madrid

After Rubens bought the estate of Het Steen near Elewijt in 1635 it became his favourite abode, and he painted many landscapes in the immediate neighbourhood. The present sketch from Oxford, which is almost entirely in grisaille, is regarded as a study for one of these, the tower being that of Het Steen. The weather is gusty and it has just been raining; the pale setting sun breaks through the clouds for a moment, casting long dark shadows and causing the damp ground and wet foliage to sparkle with radiance.

This bold, skilfully executed landscape recurs in the painting *The Tournament* in the Louvre. Another study sketch is in Berlin.

Panel, 28 : 37 cm.

Bibl.:   P. Buschmann, *Rubens en Van Dyck in het Ashmolean Museum te Oxford*, in *Onze Kunst*, XXIX, 1916, pp. 21-3; *Van Puyvelde, Esquisses*, p. 90, No. 93; G. Glück, *Die Landschaften von Peter Paul Rubens*, Vienna, 1945, p. 69, under No. 36; *Catalogue of Paintings in the Ashmolean Museum*, Oxford, s.a., p. 91, No. 387.

Prov.:   Chambers Hall (Southampton and London, 1786-1855), who bequeathed it to Oxford University.

The Ashmolean Museum, Oxford

The landscape stretches into the distance between the dark edge of the wood and the first slopes of the hilly ground to the right. A shepherd, overcome by the heat of the day, lies asleep amid his grazing flock, with a shepherdess beside him. Another shepherd, seated at the foot of a tree and also with a woman beside him, is about to play the flute, while a third invites his female companion to sit and listen to the music. The idyllic atmosphere is enhanced by the double rainbow and the evening sunshine.

Pastoral scenes had been depicted in Dutch art in the fifteenth and sixteenth centuries, especially in tapestry, but Rubens was the first to idealize them under the influence of the Venetians and especially Titian.

This picture reproduces, in broad lines and on an extended scale, the *Landscape with a Rainbow* in the Hermitage at Leningrad, which Rubens painted in the last decade of his career. Opinions are divided as to the present painting, but it is generally thought to be partly the work of Rubens's studio.

Canvas, 122:172 cm.

Bibl.: *Smith, Catalogue Raisonné*, II, p. 119; *Rooses*, IV, pp. 373, 374, No. 1185; *K.d.K., ed. Rosenberg*, p. 26; E. Kieser, *Tizians und Spaniens Einwirkungen auf die späteren Landschaften von Rubens*, in *Münchener Jahrbuch der bildenden Kunst*, N.F., VIII, 1931, p. 283; H. Herrmann, *Untersuchungen über die Landschaftsgemälde des Peter Paul Rubens*, (Dissertation), Stuttgart, 1936, pp. 56, 73, n. 65; G. Glück, *Die Landschaften von Peter Paul Rubens*, Vienna, 1945, pp. 68, 69 (under No. 34).

Prov.: Collections of King Louis XIV of France.

Musée du Louvre, Paris

CATALOGUE
Drawings

Joachim von Sandrart relates in his *Teutsche Academie*, published in 1675, that in 1627 he made a journey by tow-boat with Rubens through the Northern Provinces. The artist, reminiscing about his youth, recalled that he used to copy engravings by Hans Holbein as well as by Dürer, Tobias Stimmer and other old German masters. Among others he expressly mentioned Holbein's *Dance of Death*-series.

It was formerly supposed that the drawings in this recently discovered book were by Holbein himself, and that he made his engravings from them. The erroneous attribution to Holbein also figures on the title-page of this eighteenth-century volume. The great French collector P.J. Mariette thought in 1764 that the drawings were by Jan Boeckhorst and had belonged to Rubens, but it now appears that the contrary is the case.

I.Q. van Regteren Altena was the first to detect the hand of Rubens in these drawings. He believes them to be the master's earliest known work: they may have been done when he was twelve or thirteen years old. See Nos. 111-114.

Volume bound in small octavo, 18th-century red morocco. Pen and brush in brown ink, c. 200 : c. 150 mm.

Bibl.: P.J. Mariette, *Description Sommaire des Desseins... du Cabinet de Feu M. Crozat*, Paris, 1841, p. 89, No. 796; Idem, *Abecedario*, II, Paris, 1853-54, p. 360; Francis Douce, *Holbein's Dance of Death*, London, 1890, pp. 118-20; I.Q. van Regteren Altena, *Het vroegste werk van Rubens*, in *Mededelingen van de Koninklijke Academie voor Wetenschappen, Letteren en Schone Kunsten van België, Klasse der Schone Kunsten*, XXXIV, No. 2, 1972.

Prov.: Lord Arundel?; Jan Boeckhorst (Antwerp, 1605-68); Pierre Crozat (Paris, 1665-1740); Fleischmann; Prince Galitzine; Ambroise Firmin-Didot; Prince of Liechtenstein, sold by Mak van Waay, Amsterdam, 23 September 1969, lot 887.

Booksellers H.D. Pfann B.V., Amsterdam

pincrcuntor Angelus monstrat

Rubens drew these five figures after four woodcuts from Tobias Stimmer's (1539-89) *Neue Kunstliche Figuren Biblischer Historien*, published
at Basle in 1576. Above is an angel bringing water and bread to the
prophet Elijah, who had fled into the wilderness (*I Kings*, 19:5-6).
Below, the figure inclining forward is Abraham's servant, whom Stimmer's woodcut shows as ministering to three angels. Rubens adds the
inscription *reverenter Angelis ministrat* (*Gen.*, 18:1-15). The recumbent
figure on the right is the aged Tobit (*Tobias*, 2:10-11), and beneath
is the false prophet killed by a lion.

Sandrart, who travelled with Rubens in Holland in 1627, relates
in his note on Tobias Stimmer (*Teutsche Academie*, 1675, II, p. 254)
that, on the way between Amsterdam and Utrecht, Rubens told him
that in his early years he had copied most of the engravings in Stimmer's book. This youthful admiration left its traces in Rubens's after
life: he never forgot the robustness and resilience of Stimmer's figures
and the naturalness of his compositions.

The young Rubens not only made drawings after the
sixteenth-century German Tobias Stimmer but also after other masters
of this period such as Hans Holbein, Hans Weiditz and Jost Amman.
He also copied Israel van Meckenem and Conrad Meit. See under
No. 110.

Pen and brown ink, 206:140 mm.

Bibl.: *Evers, 1943*, pp. 95, 96; F. Lugt, *Rubens and Stimmer*, in *The Art Quarterly*,
VI, 1943, pp. 99-115; *Burchard-d'Hulst*, 1956, p. 28, No. 1.

Prov.: Bequeathed to the City of Rotterdam by F.J.O. Boymans (1767-1847).

Boymans-van Beuningen Museum, Rotterdam

– after Tobias Stimmer

E.K.J. Rezniček rediscovered this fluent drawing in the art trade in Florence. It is one of a series of sheets dating from Rubens's youth, executed before his departure for Italy in 1600 and probably, as J.S. Held supposed, before his twentieth year. Like the preceding drawing, it is copied after a woodcut in Tobias Stimmer's *Neue Kunstliche Figuren Biblischer Historien*, published at Basle in 1576. The sheet illustrates the grace and delicacy with which Rubens interpreted his model. It is notable, in particular, how he accentuated the dynamic effect of Samson with his impetuous stride and the spiral drapery of his cloak. See under No. 110.

Pen and brown ink, 157:123 mm.

Bibl.:   *Evers, 1943*, pp. 95, 96; F. Lugt, *Rubens and Stimmer*, in *The Art Quarterly*, VI, 1943, pp. 99-114; *Held*, pp. 155, 156, No. 156.
Prov.:   Purchased at Florence by E.K.J. Rezniček; sold at Sotheby's, London, successively on 1 July 1965, lot 162, and 21 March 1973, lot 11.

André Leysen Collection, Antwerp

Each of these women represents Eve in a different attitude. The second, third and fourth are copied from woodcuts in Tobias Stimmer's *Neue Kunstliche Figuren Biblischer Historien*, published at Basle in 1576. They represent (upper right) Eve under the forbidden tree, (lower left) the creation of Eve, and (lower right) the expulsion from paradise. The upper left figure is from a woodcut by Jost Amman in *Opera Josephi. De Antiquitatibus judaicis*, published at Frankfurt on Main in 1580. In the woodcut Eve has an apple in her hand.

Comparison with the models shows how Rubens strove to perfect the modelling of these female nudes. See under No. 110.

The right-hand side of the sheet is cut off irregularly. Pen and brown ink, 174:128 mm.

Bibl.:   *Evers, 1943*, pp. 95, 96; F. Lugt, *Rubens and Stimmer*, in *The Art Quarterly*, VI, 1943, pp. 99-115; *Lugt, Louvre, Ecole flamande, II, 1949*, p. 34, No. 1116.

Prov.:   Unknown.

Cabinet des dessins, Musée du Louvre, Paris

FOUR MALE FIGURES – after Tobias Stimmer and Hendrick **114**
Goltzius

The man seen from behind, upper left, is copied from the executioner
with a rod in *The Scourging of Christ*, an engraving by the Dutch artist
Hendrick Goltzius. The drawing was made before Rubens left for Italy
in 1600, so that the engraving, which bears the date 1597, must have
become known in the Southern Netherlands very soon thereafter. The
other three figures are from Tobias Stimmer's *Neue Kunstliche Figuren
Biblischer Historien* of 1576. The man, upper right, is a musician accompanying the temple singers; the figure, lower left, is a man bending
over Elisha's tomb, while the last figure represents the aged Samuel
on his knees, offering sacrifice. See under No. 110.

Pen and brown ink, 189 : 116 mm.

Bibl.:   *Evers, 1943*, pp. 95, 96; F. Lugt, *Rubens and Stimmer*, in *The Art Quarterly*,
VI, 1943, pp. 99-115; *Lugt, Louvre, Ecole flamande, II, 1949*, p. 35, No. 1121.

Prov.: Unknown.

Cabinet des dessins, Musée du Louvre, Paris

This drawing is clearly from Rubens's Italian period, and was probably executed in his first years there. The statue is seen against a wall on which it throws dark shadows. The tree-trunk between the feet is a common feature in late antique statuary. Rubens drew the statue from below, so that the head is much foreshortened. Below, on the right, the left foot is repeated on a larger scale, with the sandal in careful detail. After the statue was drawn by Rubens it came into the possession of the Earl of Arundel.

Later, c. 1623-24, Rubens used this drawing with slight modifications for the figure of Cronos in *The Council of the Gods*, a painting in the Medici cycle executed for the Palais du Luxembourg in Paris and now in the Louvre.

Several other drawings by Rubens after antique sculpture are known from this period: *Standing Roman with toga*, Institut Néerlandais, Paris; *Mars and Venus*, Hermitage, Leningrad; *Sleeping Hermaphrodite*, Fogg Art Museum, Cambridge, Mass.; and a *Richly draped Standing Woman*, British Museum, London. See No. 116.

Black chalk, 552 : 361 mm.

Bibl.: *Bock-Rosenberg*, p. 251, No. 10.601; *Burchard-d'Hulst, 1963*, pp. 27-9, No. 12.

Prov.: Acquired in 1920.

Staatliche Museen Preußischer Kulturbesitz, Kupferstichkabinett, Berlin-West

In Rubens's time the Laocoon group, discorered in 1506, was in the Belvedere at the Vatican; it is now in the Vatican Museum. Artists and collectors, attracted by its beauty and expressiveness, endeavoured to obtain casts or copies of it. It is not certain whether Rubens's drawing was made from the sculpture itself or from a plaster cast. Whereas other artists drew antique statuary from an 'ideal' distance, Rubens drew the Laocoon from close up and from a low viewpoint. Clearly he was most interested in the musculature of the trunk, which also explains the three-quarter length.

Rubens used this drawing, in reverse, for a man in armour in *The Raising of the Brazen Serpent*, c. 1630, National Gallery, London. Figures inspired by the Laocoon can also be seen in *The Crowning with Thorns*, chapel of the hospital at Grasse, *Hercules and Omphale*, Louvre, Paris (both of 1602) and *The Massacre of the Innocents*, 1639. Sometimes Rubens used only part of the drawing, as in the torso of the Bad Thief in the *Coup de lance*, Antwerp Museum. See No. 115.

Black chalk, 457:297 mm.

Bibl.: *Burchard-d'Hulst, 1963*, pp. 31-3, No. 15; Victor W. Miesel, *Rubens's Study Drawings after Ancient Sculpture*, in *Gazette des Beaux-Arts*, May-June 1963, p. 311 e.a.; G. Fubini and J.S. Held, *Padre Resta's Rubens Drawings after Ancient Sculpture*, in *Master Drawings*, 1964, II, No. 2, p. 131; J. Müller Hofstede, *Beiträge zum zeichnerischen Werk von Rubens*, in *Wallraf-Richartz-Jahrbuch*, 1965, XXVII, p. 270.

Prov.: Sir Thomas Lawrence (Londen, 1769-1830); Samuel Woodburn (London, 1786-1853); sale, Christie's, London, 1860, lot 914. Acquired in London, 1874.

Kupferstichkabinett der Staatlichen Kunstsammlungen, Dresden, DDR

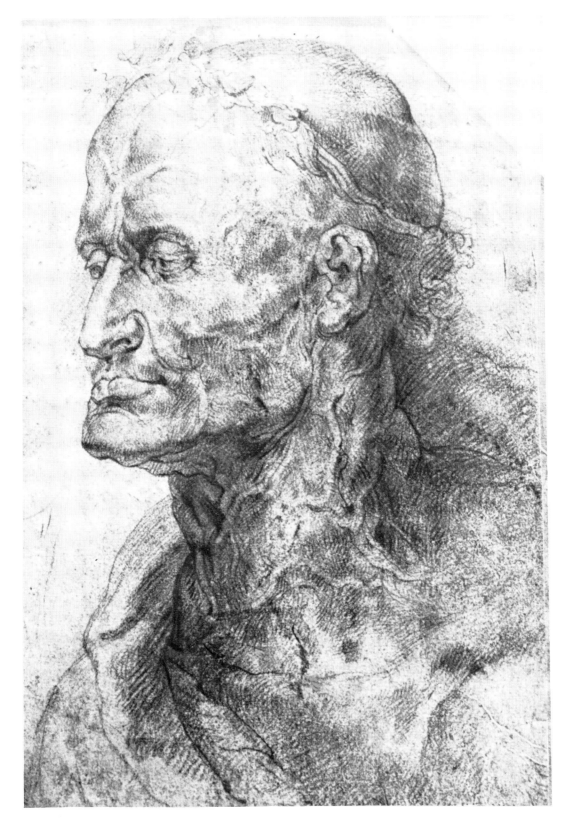

Head of an aged man, almost in left profile. A lightly twined laurel wreath rests on his bare skull. His gaze is somewhat introspective, but strength of will is shown in his tight lips and powerfully protruding chin. Extreme care is devoted to anatomical features such as the structure of the skull and the veins of the neck.

This drawing, previously unknown, was published as by Rubens in 1968 by M. Jaffé, who believed it to be of the Roman emperor Servius Sulpicius Galba; however, comparison with other portraits of Galba throws doubt on this. On stylistic grounds the drawing may be dated to the first years of Rubens's stay in Italy, and it most probably derives directly or indirectly from a model by Leonardo da Vinci.

Right upper corner missing. Red chalk, 233 : 155 mm.

Bibl.:   M. Jaffé, *Rubens in Italy, Part II*, in *The Burlington Magazine*, CX, 1968, pp. 184-7; Cat. Exh. *Rubens en zijn tijd, tekeningen uit Belgische verzamelingen*, Rubenshouse, Antwerp, 1971, pp. 75, 76, No. 57.

Prov.:   Purchased in the art market, *c.* 1950.

Private collection, Ghent

A drawing of Rubens's Italian period after Leonardo da Vinci's fresco, begun in 1505, for the council chamber of the Palazzo Vecchio in Florence. The fresco, which for various reasons was never finished, represented *The Battle of Anghiari*, a victory won against the Milanese in 1441. It is generally supposed that Leonardo painted only the central part depicting four horsemen fighting for the standard, with three figures on the ground. Both the fresco and the cartoon are lost.

Various sixteenth-century copies, in the form of paintings, drawings or engravings, the complete accuracy of which is much disputed, have afforded a popular subject of study for many painters from Raphael to Delacroix. Rubens's drawing is not directly based on the fresco, which was destroyed in 1557, nor can it be an exact version of the lost cartoon. Although of limited documentary value for the reconstruction of Leonardo's composition, it renders the spirit of the fight better than any earlier copy.

Rubens devoted much care to this drawing, both the modelling of the forms and the various details. His workmanship is seen at its best in the pen-strokes and colouring which make the drawing inimitably true to life. The purpose for which it was executed is unknown.

Enlarged on all four sides. Black chalk, pen and brown ink, washed and heightened with body-colour, 452:637 mm.

Bibl.:   *Reiset*, No. 565; *Rooses*, V, pp. 206, 207, No. 1395; *Glück-Haberditsl*, p. 29, No. 9; K.F. Suter, *Das Rätsel von Leonardo's Schlachtenbild*, Strasbourg, 1937; *Lugt, Louvre, Ecole flamande, II, 1949*, pp. 29, 30, No. 1084; *Held*, pp. 157-9, No. 161.

Prov.:   Count C.G. Tessin (Stockholm, 1695-1770); Queen Ulrica Louisa of Sweden, then her daughter Princess Sophia Albertina; Count G.H. Steinbock (Stockholm, 1764-1833); Count Nils Barck (Paris, Madrid, 1820-96), who sold it to the Louvre in 1852.

Cabinet des Dessins, Musée du Louvre, Paris

Raphael

Vexed at man's sinful life, God resolved to destroy humanity by visiting a flood upon the earth. Only the righteous Noah found favour in his eyes and was spared, with his family, to become the ancestor of a new race of men (*Genesis*, 6-9).

God the Father, hovering in the air and borne by three cherubs, is seen giving orders to Noah to build the ark in which he is to escape the deluge. Noah, kneeling in front of his house, clasps one of his three sons to his breast; his wife stands in the doorway with their other two sons.

Several drawings by Rubens after Raphael are known. The present one was executed with great care during the first years of Rubens's stay in Italy, after an engraving of Raphael's composition by Marcantonio Raimondi.

Sheet damaged on the left. Red chalk, heightened with body colour in places. 315 : 256 mm.

Bibl.: *Glück-Haberditzl*, p. 29, Ab. 11; *Lugt, Louvre, Ecole flamande, II, 1949*, p. 21, No. 1036; *Burchard-d'Hulst, 1956*, p. 40, No. 21; *Burchard-d'Hulst, 1963*, pp. 41, 42, No. 22.

Prov.: E. Jabach (Paris, 1607/10-95). Belonged to the collection sold by E. Jabach to King Louis XIV of France on 29 March 1671.

Cabinet des dessins, Musée du Louvre, Paris

During a stay in Rome shortly after his arrival in Italy, Rubens visited the Sixtine Chapel, where he copied paintings by Michelangelo. Thus he drew various sybils and prophets, including Isaiah, after the ceiling frescoes.

These are painstaking and accurate copies, and thus do not display the exuberance with which Rubens later handled pen or chalk. None the less, he reproduced with great clarity the monumental character of Michelangelo's figures. Thanks to the combined use of black and red chalk, which was much in vogue at the time in Florence and Rome, he was able to prevent these large sheets from presenting too severe an appearance.

Black and red chalk, 465 : 365 mm.

Bibl.: *Reiset*, No. 569; *Rooses*, V, p. 194, No. 1366; *Glück-Haberditzl*, p. 30, No. 14; *Lugt, Louvre, Ecole flamande II, 1949*, pp. 22, 23, No. 1047.

Prov.: E. Jabach; King Louis XIV of France. The drawing was most probably one of the works bought by the King from Jabach on 29 March 1671.

Cabinet des dessins, Musée du Louvre, Paris

The naked Christ stands on the left in the waters of the Jordan; his garment is held by three angels. John the Baptist, on the bank, pours water on Christ's head and looks up to heaven, whence the Holy Spirit descends in the form of a dove. To the right several men, some standing and others sitting, are disrobing before stepping into the river and being baptized. A group of women is in the distance.

The drawing is squared, indicating that it was intended to be reproduced on a large scale. It was in fact a study for *The Baptism of Christ*, one of three pictures ordered by Duke Vincenzo I for the Santissima Trinità at Mantua (see p. 41) and now in the Antwerp Museum. The canvas does not follow the drawing literally: for instance, a group of cherubs is added above Christ's head, the women are disposed differently and the young man leaning against a tree in the foreground is omitted.

It is accepted that the group formed by Christ and John was influenced by Raphael's fresco in the Vatican *Logge*. However, Rubens was mainly inspired by Michengelo's *Bathers (The Battle of Cascina)*, although no single figure is taken literally from that work. The seated man holding his foot is an adaptation of the antique *Spinario (Man with a Thorn)*, while the one pulling off his shirt is inspired by the *Farnese Hercules*; the youth in the centre foreground probably also derives from an antique sculpture.

Two strips of paper added by Rubens himself at the top. Black chalk, heightened with body colour, 477:766 mm.

Bibl.: *Smith, Catalogue Raisonné*, II, pp. 262, 263, under No. 887; *Rooses*, II, p. 5; *Idem*, V, pp. 153, 154, No. 1343; E. Michel, *Rubens, sa vie, son œuvre et son temps*, Paris, 1900, pl. VIII; F.M. Haberditzl, *Studien über Rubens*, in *Wiener Jahrbuch*, XXX, 1912, p. 264; *Glück-Haberditzl*, p. 54, No. 50; *Glück*, p. 3, No. 5; *Lugt, Louvre, Ecole flamande, II, 1949*, pp. 12, 13, No. 1009; *Held*, p. 98, No. 11; *Burchard-d'Hulst, 1963*, pp. 53-5, No. 29.

Prov.: E. Jabach (Paris, 1607/10-95). Part of the collection sold by Jabach to King Louis XIV of France on 29 March 1671.

Cabinet des dessins, Musée du Louvre, Paris

Full-length 'life' study of a young halberdier. Rubens paid special attention to the folds of the drapery, with its effect of movement and shades of light. The drawing is related to one of the figures in *The Gonzaga Family Adoring the Holy Trinity*, painted in 1604-05 for the Santissima Trinità at Mantua (see p. 41). Apart from its intrinsic quality it is of especial value as 'life' drawings of Rubens's Italian period are rare.

Black, white and red chalk, a little pen and brown ink, lightly washed, 407:260 mm.

Bibl.:   L. Ozzola, *Restauri di un Rubens a Mantova*, in *Bolletino d'Arte del Ministero della Publica Istruzione*, 1952, p. 100; M. Jaffé, *The Interest of Rubens in Annibale and Agostino Carracci*, in *The Burlington Magazine*, XCIX, 1957, p. 379, No. 17; *Held*, p. 127, No. 72; M. Jaffé, *Rubens as a Draughtsman*, in *The Burlington Magazine*, CVII, 1965, p. 376; Frances Huemer, *Some Observations on Rubens' Mantua Altarpiece*, in *The Art Bulletin*, 48, 1966, p. 84; H. Vlieghe, in *Openbaar Kunstbezit in Vlaanderen*, VII, 1969, No. 15; Cat. Exh. *Rubens en zijn tijd, tekeningen uit Belgische Verzamelingen*, Rubenshouse, Antwerp, 1971, pp. 78, 79, No. 59.

Prov.:   P.H. Lankrink (London, 1628-92); J. Van Haecken (London, 1699?-1749), sold in London (Langford), 17-20 January 1758; M. Jaffé, Cambridge, sold by him at Sotheby's, London, 11 November 1965, lot 56, bought by the Royal Library.

Print-room, Royal Albert I Library, Brussels

When the church authorities rejected the panel painting executed by Rubens in 1607 for the high altar of S. Maria in Vallicella in Rome, he replaced it by three other paintings on slate (see under No. 15). The original plan had combined two themes: the glorification of St. Gregory the Great, patron of the church, and the adoration of a miraculous picture of the Virgin. In the new version these were separated: the adoration of the picture became the principal theme, and the sole subject of the central painting for the high altar. For this composition Rubens made a drawing, now in the Albertina at Vienna, and an oil sketch after it which is now in the Vienna Academy (see No. 16).

The purpose of the present sheet is disputed. Some believe that it was part of the preparatory work for the painting in S. Maria in Vallicella: in that case it must have been executed before the oil sketch, as the latter already contains every element of the finished painting, and after the Vienna drawing for compositional reasons. Others think the sheet was not part of that process but was intended for a different painting. Its authenticity has also been called in question. F. Lugt accepted it as by Rubens, though he was not much impressed by its quality; J.S. Held and M. Jaffé rejected it, the latter in favour of another version in the Pushkin Museum in Moscow, which is undoubtedly superior.

Black and red chalk, some contours reworked in silverpoint, 449:346 mm.

Bibl.:   *Rooses*, V, p. 229, No. 1432; *Glück-Haberditzl*, p. 35, No. 55; *Evers, 1943*, p. 115; *Lugt, Louvre, Ecole flamande, II, 1949*, pp. 11, 12, No. 1008; *Held*, p. 101, under No. 17; M. Jaffé, *Peter Paul Rubens and the Oratorian Fathers*, in *Proporzioni*, IV, [1959], p. 38, Appendix.

Prov.:   Unknown.

Cabinet des dessins, Musée du Louvre, Paris

These heads are among the numerous studies drawn by Rubens after
North European models of the fifteenth and sixteenth centuries. The
head in the upper right corner was repeated, rapidly sketched, in a
slightly different attitude. Some of the women are drawn as far as
the shoulders, but Rubens was chiefly interested in the head-dresses.

Friedrich Winkler pointed out that the head in the lower left corner
is copied from the left-hand panel of Rogier van der Weyden's Bladelin
altarpiece, while J.S. Held observed that the first four heads above
on the left and the last two below are based on Heinrich Vogtherr's
Kunstbüchlin, a book of models first published in 1537 and afterwards
in several editions in different languages, the last dating from 1610.
Vogtherr himself probably took his models from the work of early
sixteenth-century Antwerp masters, such as Jan de Beer, or perhaps
from Jacob Cornelisz. The present drawing must have been done
shortly after Rubens's return from Italy.

Pen and brown ink, 202 : 314 mm.

Bibl.:   *Burchard-d'Hulst, 1956*, p. 30, No. 6; *Held*, p. 159, No. 162; J.S. Held, *Rubens'
         Designs for Sepulchral Monuments*, in *The Art Quarterly*, XXIII, 1960, pp. 247-70;
         Burchard-d'Hulst, 1963, pp. 15, 16, No. 3.

Prov.:   Probably purchased by Duke Charles I of Brunswick (1713-80).

Herzog-Anton-Ulrich-Museum, Brunswick

The lifeless Abel lies on his back, his face towards the spectator and his feet on the altar of sacrifice; his right arm lies along his body, while his left arm is bent above the shoulder. The jawbone with which Cain has killed him lies between his legs and on his belly. Two trees can be seen in the distance (*Genesis*, 4:8-15).

As E. Christopher Norris pointed out, this is a copy after Michiel Coxcie's (1499-1592) painting *Cain condemned by the Lord* in the Prado, Madrid. Another drawing by Rubens, probably 'from life' and now in the Louvre, resembles the figure of the slave in Tintoretto's *Miracle of St. Mark* in details such as the right arm, but remains close to Coxcie's Abel as far as the head is concerned.

The attitude of the slain Abel, borrowed from Coxcie by Rubens, influenced other painters also, such as Johann Liss in his *Lamentation over Abel*.

Left upper corner of the sheet cut off and replaced. Red chalk, reworked with the tip of the brush in red and heightened with white, 213 : 208 mm.

Bibl.: *Burchard-d'Hulst, 1956*, p. 39, No. 19; *Burchard-d'Hulst, 1963*, pp. 60, 61, No. 33.

Prov.: P.H. Lankrink (London, 1628-92); J. Richardson Sr. (London, 1665-1745); Sir Joshua Reynolds (London, 1723-92); T. Banks (London, 1735-1805); Sir E.J. Paynter (London, 1836-1919), sold at Sotheby's, London, 25 April 1858, lot 189; Charles Clarke, bequeathed in 1935 to Dr L.C.G. Clarke (Cambridge, 1881-1960), who bequeathed it to the Museum.

The Fitzwilliam Museum, Cambridge

This drawing was previously thought to represent either Samson slaying the Philistines or Cain killing Abel. J. Müller Hofstede pointed out, probably rightly, that it is a study for *The Murder of Abel*, a painting of *c.* 1608-09 in the possession of Count A. Seilern in London.

Pen and brown ink and brown wash over preliminary work in black and red chalk, 268 : 183 mm.

Bibl.:   J.S. Held, *Comments on Rubens' Beginnings*, in *Miscellanea D. Roggen*, 1957, pp. 134, 135; *Held*, pp. 97, 98, No. 10; *Burchard-d'Hulst, 1963*, pp. 81-3, No. 48; J. Müller Hofstede, Review of *Burchard-d'Hulst, 1963*, in *Master Drawings*, 1966, No. 4, p. 443, No. 48; [Count A. Seilern], *Flemish Paintings and Drawings at 56, Princes Gate, London, SW7, Addenda*, London, 1969, pp. 8-10, under No. 298.

Prov.:   J. Richardson Sr. (London, 1665-1745); Thomas Hudson (London, 1701-79); Henry Oppenheimer (London, 1859-1932), sold at Christie's, London, 10-14 July 1936, lot 238B, and bought by I.Q. van Regteren Altena for the Fodor collection.

Historisch Museum, Amsterdam

More than half the sheet is occupied by two figures, a young man and an old woman, both in half-length, their bodies turned three-quarters to the right. Both are looking upward; the young man's head faces the spectator. In the right corner is a study of a man's head in a turban.

J.S. Held regards the two main figures as studies for *The Adoration of the Shepherds* in St. Philip Neri's church at Fermo, consecrated in 1607 (see No. 17). According to L. Burchard and R.-A. d'Hulst, however, they are connected rather with the painting of the same title in St. Paul's at Antwerp, executed by Rubens shortly after his return from Italy; the turbaned head, these authors suggest, may be a study for St. Joseph.

Sheet restored, upper left. Pen and brown ink and brown wash, 140:151 mm.

Bibl.: J.S. Held, *Rubens' Pen Drawings*, in *Magazine of Art*, 1951, p. 290; *Held*, p. 101, No. 18; *Burchard-d'Hulst, 1963*, pp. 73, 74, No. 41.

Prov.: Bought for the Fodor collection by I.Q. van Regteren Altena at the Mensing sale, Amsterdam, 27-29 April 1937, lot 187.

Historisch Museum, Amsterdam

An old serving-woman lays before Salome a dish with the Baptist's head on it. Salome takes hold of the Baptist's tongue, with which he had rebuked Herod for marrying Herodias, Salome's mother (*Matthew*, 14:1-12). The group in this drawing figured in *The Beheading of John the Baptist*, a lost painting of 1609, known only from copies. Possibly the drawing was not a sketch for the picture but a reminiscence of it.

On the back of the sheet is another scene with a severed head: a rapid sketch in pen and brown ink showing David in profile, holding Goliath's head in his outstretched hands. Thus both sides depict a scene involving a severed head.

Upper corners of the sheet cut off and restored. Pen and brown ink, and brown wash, 183 : 130 mm.

Bibl.: *Burchard-d'Hulst, 1963*, pp. 74, 75, No. 42.

Prov.: Henry Oppenheimer (London, 1859-1932), sold at Christie's, London, 10-14 July 1936, lot 238A, bought by I.Q. van Regteren Altena for the Fodor collection.

Historisch Museum, Amsterdam

A preliminary sketch, representing the cutting of Samson's hair, for a painting of *c.* 1610 which belonged to Rubens's friend and patron Nicolaas Rockox, mayor of Amsterdam, and which is now in a private collection (see No. 20).

Pen and brown ink and brown wash, 164 : 162 mm.

Bibl.: L. Burchard, *Die Skizzen des jungen Rubens*, in *Sitzungsberichte der Kunstgeschicht-lichen Gesellschaft*, Berlin, 8 October 1926, p. 3, No. 20; L. Burchard in *Glück*, p. 382; H.G. Evers, *"Frierende Venus" von Rubens*, in *Pantheon*, IV, 1942, pp. 83-6; *Evers, 1943*, pp. 151, 162; *Burchard-d'Hulst, 1956*, pp. 46, 47, No. 32; *Held*, p. 103, No. 24; *Burchard-d'Hulst, 1963*, pp. 79, 80, No. 46.

Prov.: Unknown.

Prof. Dr. I.Q. van Regteren Altena, Amsterdam

Study, from the living model, of a naked young man. His body is bent backwards and his muscles are tensed by the effort of pushing up a heavy weight. Rubens seems to have copied his pose from an antique marble group of *Two Wrestlers*, now in Florence.

A figure related to this drawing appears in *The Raising of the Cross* at Grasse (1602) and in the painting of the same subject in Antwerp Cathedral (1610-11); Rubens also used it on later occasions. Its date is disputed: some place it in Rubens's early Italian period, others believe it to have been a study for *The Raising of the Cross*, painted soon after his return to Antwerp.

Lower right part of sheet slightly damaged. Black chalk, heightened with white, 315 : 367 mm.

Bibl.: S. Colvin, *Drawings in the University Galleries*, Oxford, 1903-7, III, 2, Pl. 20; F.M. Haberditzl, *Studiën über Rubens*, in *Wiener Jahrbuch*, 1911-12, p. 260; R. Oldenbourg, *Rubens in Italien*, in *Berliner Jahrbuch*, 1916, p. 278; *Glück-Haberditzl*, p. 33, No. 45; K.T. Parker, *Catalogue of the Collection of Drawings in the Ashmolean Museum*, Oxford, 1938, I, pp. 85, 86, No. 200; *Burchard*, pp. 58, 59, No. 52; *Burchard-d'Hulst, 1956*, pp. 32, 33, No. 9; M. Jaffé, *Rubens' Drawings at Antwerp*, in *The Burlington Magazine*, XCVIII, 1956, p. 317; *Burchard-d'Hulst, 1963*, pp. 97, 98, No. 57.

Prov.: P.H. Lankrink (London, 1628-92). Bequeathed to Oxford University by Chambers Hall (Southampton and London, 1786-1855).

The Ashmolean Museum, Oxford

Study 'from life' of a naked young man pushing a load upwards. His left arm forms a diagonal with his body and right leg. Rubens re-drew the left leg in a more lifelike position, and also reworked the right foot.

The study was used for a figure in the centre panel of *The Raising of the Cross* (*c.* 1610-11), which adorned the high altar of St. Walburga's church in Antwerp (now destroyed) and is now in the cathedral there. However, the figure in the painting is in armour and his head is less in profile. See No. 132.

The right upper and lower corners of the original sheet are missing. Black chalk, heightened with white, 488 : 315 mm.

Bibl.:   *Burchard-d'Hulst, 1956*, pp. 48, 49, No. 35; *Held*, p. 129, No. 76; *Burchard-d'Hulst, 1963*, p. 96, No. 56.

Prov.:   Versteegh, 1823; Sir Thomas Lawrence (London, 1769-1830). Probably from the collection of King William II of the Netherlands.

Her Majesty the Queen of the Netherlands

A study 'from life' which pays attention to the movement of the body as well as its posture; the skin and muscles are rendered with precision. Like the previous drawing (No. 131), this is a study for one of the figures in the centre panel of *The Raising of the Cross* (1610-11), formerly in St. Walburga's and now in Antwerp cathedral. The man is lifting with both hands the crossbeam that is to support Christ's body. The touches in Chinese ink seem to have been added later by another hand, perhaps that of the painter Jacob de Wit, who is said to have once owned the drawing.

Faded yellow paper. Black chalk, heightened with white and reworked with Chinese ink, 465 : 320 mm.

Bibl.: *Burchard-d'Hulst, 1956*, p. 61, No. 36; *Burchard-d'Hulst, 1963*, pp. 98, 99, No. 58.

Prov.: Jacob de Wit?; Simon Fokke?; Ploss van Amstel?; Versteegh, 1823; Sir Thomas Lawrence (London, 1769-1830); De Kat, sold at Rotterdam, 4 March 1867, lot 104; J. de Clercq, Amsterdam, 1867.

Mr C.P. van Eeghen, Amsterdam

The body of Christ lies in a cave, on a shroud spread over a rectangular stone. Mary, supported by St. John, holds up the body from behind, while Joseph of Arimathea lifts the bottom end of the shroud with both hands and with his teeth. Behind are Mary Magdalen, Mary the wife of Cleophas, and Nicodemus; a youth lights the scene with a torch.

This drawing, first ascribed to Rubens by I.Q. van Regteren Altena, derives from an engraving of the same title by Giovanni Battista Franco (1498?-1561), with the same composition and the motif of a man holding the shroud between his teeth. This motif also occurs in other works by Rubens, such as *The Descent from the Cross* in Antwerp cathedral, or an oil sketch in the Rennes Museum for the painting of the same subject in the Museum at Lille.

Pen and brown and grey ink, brown and grey wash, 324:409 mm.

Bibl.: I.Q. van Regteren Altena, *Rubens as a Draughtsman – 1. Relation to Italian Art*, in *The Burlington Magazine*, LXXVI, 1940, p. 199; *Held*, pp. 94, 95, No. 4; *Burchard-d'Hulst, 1963*, pp. 64-6, No. 36.

Prov.: Bequeathed to the City of Rotterdam by F.J.O. Boymans (1767-1847).

Boymans-van Beuningen Museum, Rotterdam

Rubens Tiré du Cabinet de Crozat.   1735.

Full-length drawing of a young man, illuminated from the lower right. His right leg is bent back, as is his right arm, with which he appears to be grasping for support. His left arm, for which an alternative pose is offered, is raised and stretched out in a defensive attitude. As the sheet was too small for the complete figure, Rubens also drew this arm separately.

A study for the figure of Job in the left-hand panel of the Job triptych, commissioned in 1612 by the Musicians' Guild of Brussels for their altar in St. Nicholas's church. The triptych was destroyed in the French bombardement of 1695. The panel showed Job on a dunghill, reviled by his wife and tormented by devils.

Sheet cut down on the right and restored. Black chalk heightened with white, 570:444 mm.

Bibl.:   *Burchard-d'Hulst, 1963*, pp. 119-21, No. 72; J. Müller Hofstede, Review of
            Burchard-d'Hulst, 1963, in *Master Drawings*, 1966, No. 4, pp. 447, 450.

Prov.:   Pierre Crozat (Paris, 1665-1740); Count C.G. Tessin (Stockholm, 1695-1770); acquired by the Royal Museum in 1735.

Nationalmuseum, Stockholm

Study 'from life' of a young man. This drawing has generally been regarded as a study for the youth accompanying the saint in *The Miracles of St. Francis Xavier*, painted by Rubens in 1619-20 for the Jesuit church at Antwerp and now in Vienna. M. Jaffé considers, however, that the youth in the painting and in the modello preceding it bears little or no resemblance to the drawing. He dates the latter *c.* 1613-14 and believes it to be a study for the Apostle John.

Black chalk, heightened with white, 493 : 288 mm.

Bibl.: *Glück-Haberditzl*, p. 45, No. 123; M. Jaffé, *The Interest of Rubens in Annibale and Agostino Carracci: further notes*, in *The Burlington Magazine*, XCIX, 1957, pp. 375-9, n. 5; *Burchard-d'Hulst, 1963*, p. 181, under No. 114; *Vlieghe, Saints*, II, p. 33, No. 104f.

Prov.: C. Ricketts (London, 1886-1931) and H.C. Shannon (London, 1865-1937). Bequeathed by H.C. Shannon to the Fitswilliam Museum in 1937.

The Fitzwilliam Museum, Cambridge

A sketch for the right-hand panel of *The Descent from the Cross*, commissioned by the Arquebusiers' Guild for their altar in Antwerp cathedral. The centre panel of this altarpiece was painted in 1611-12, the side panels in 1613-14. The composition, comprising the figures of Mary, Joseph, Anna the prophetess and Simeon, differs somewhat in the drawing as compared with the painting: in this side panel, Anna stands between Mary and Simeon. The posture of the figures is also somewhat different, e.g. Joseph is seen here almost in full profile.

The drawing is a fragment of a larger sheet that originally included another study for the same *Presentation* (coll. Count A. Seilern, London) and several studies for *The Visitation* on the left-hand panel of the Antwerp *Descent from the Cross* (Musée Bonnat, Bayonne).

On the verso is a fragment of a study in black chalk for a *Raising of the Cross*.

Pen and brown ink and brown wash, 214:142 mm.

Bibl.: *Held*, p. 105, No. 28; *Burchard-d'Hulst, 1963*, pp. 101-3, under No. 60.

Prov.: Presented to the Metropolitan Museum in 1952 by Mr. and Mrs. Janos Scholz.

The Metropolitan Museum of Art, Gift of Mr. and Mrs. Janos Scholz, 1952, New York

The drawing shows the whole company of saints worshipping the Holy Trinity. Mary is at Christ's feet and behind her is a group in which Peter, Paul and John the Baptist can be recognized by their attributes. At the same level as the Apostles is a group of female saints on a stretch of cloud. Below is a group of Franciscans, Dominicans and other male saints and martyrs, including St. Sebastian with his arrows, St. George in armour, St. Lawrence with his grid and Pope St. Gregory, his tiara beside him on the ground.

A study for an engraving that was executed by Theodoor Galle as an illustration to the *Breviarium Romanum* published by Balthasar Moretus in 1614. The composition derives from Venetian models and especially Titian's *Triumph of the Holy Trinity* (1554), which Rubens may have seen during his visit to Spain in 1603; he could also have known it from Cornelis Cort's engraving of 1566.

An oil sketch of the same subject, related to this drawing, is in the Boymans-van Beuningen Museum at Rotterdam (see No. 29). It is doubtful, however, that it was also made for the purpose of the engraving.

Drawing retraced with the burin. Pen and brown ink and brown wash, 295:200 mm.

Bibl.: *Rooses*, V, p. 61, under No. 1259; L. Burchard, *Skizzen des jungen Rubens*, in *Sitzungsberichte der Kunstgeschichtlichen Gesellschaft*, Berlin, 8 October 1926, p. 3, No. 23; *Glück-Haberditzl*, p. 29, No. 7; *Evers, 1943*, pp. 218, 219; *Lugt, Louvre, Ecole flamande, II, 1949*, p. 12, under No. 1009; Cat. Exh. *Rotterdam, 1953-54*, pp. 43, 44, under No. 13; *Burchard-d'Hulst, 1956*, p. 56, under No. 48; *Held*, pp. 26, 98 (under No. 11); *Burchard-d'Hulst*, 1963, p. 54 (under No. 29), p. 114 (under No. 68); *d'Hulst, 1968*, p. 91, under No. 3; *Vlieghe, Saints*, I, p. 28, under No. 1; J.R. Judson and C. Van de Velde, *Book Illustrations and Title-pages, Corpus Rubenianum Ludwig Burchard*, XXI, Brussels, 1977 (in preparation).

Prov.: G. Huquier (Orléans and Paris, 1695-1772); sold by Yver at Amsterdam, 14 September 1761 ff., lot 553, from the Uilenbroek collection, Amsterdam; Count Moriz von Fries (Vienna, 1776-1826).

Graphische Sammlung Albertina, Vienna

Rubens

Almost the whole right-hand half of the sheet is taken up by a study of the naked legs of a man seen from behind, who is walking forward with his right leg raised. Above on the left is a study of a bent right arm, the hand grasping an object. Below, a study of the arms of a man with his face buried in his hands. This was used for a man shielding his eyes against the dazzling light in *The Conversion of St. Paul*, in the possession of Count A. Seilern in London. As the painting dates from *c.* 1615, the drawing is certainly not later and may be dated *c.* 1611-14.

Similar studies of arms and legs by Rubens can be seen in the Victoria and Albert Museum in London, the Dresden Print-Room and the National Museum in Stockholm.

Black chalk with traces of heightening whith white, 350:240 mm.

Bibl.:   *Burchard-d'Hulst, 1956*, p. 65, No. 63; *Held*, p. 110, No. 79.

Prov.:   P.H. Lankrink (London, 1628-92); Sir J.C. Robinson (London, 1824-1913); E. Wauters (Paris, 1846-1933), sold by Fr. Muller & Co., Amsterdam, 15-16 June 1926, lot 169; F. Koenigs (Haarlem, 1881-1941). Presented to the Boymans Museum Foundation by D.G. van Beuningen in 1940.

Boymans-van Beuningen Museum, Rotterdam

St. John and Joseph of Arimathea support the dead body of Christ, while Nicodemus, holding a corner of the shroud, looks up at the weeping Virgin. Two women's heads can be seen on Mary's left. A youth in the centre of the group holds up a torch. The scene takes place in a cave, and a branch of a tree is seen through an opening in the roof.

This drawing, which dates from *c.* 1615, shows the influence of Caravaggio's *Burial of Christ* in the Vatican. A paraphrase of that work, painted by Rubens, is now in the Ottawa Museum (see No. 32).

Pen and brown ink and brown wash, 233 : 153 mm.

Bibl.:   *Evers, 1943*, p. 139; *Held*, pp. 109, 110, No. 37; *Burchard-d'Hulst, 1963*, pp. 68-70, No. 38.

Prov.:   T. Hudson (London, 1701-79); Sir Thomas Lawrence (London, 1769-1830); Jacob de Vos Jbzn (Amsterdam, 1803-82), sold at Amsterdam, 22 May 1883, lot 143; W. Pitcairn Knowles (Rotterdam, 1820-94), sold at Amsterdam, 25 June 1891, lot 202.

Rijksprentenkabinet, Rijksmuseum, Amsterdam

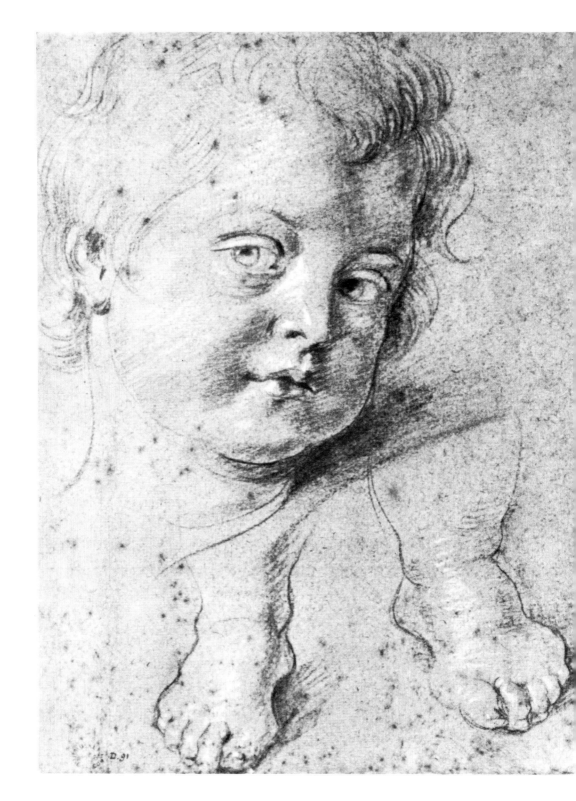

It is generally supposed that one of Rubens's children posed for this drawing, which authors date variously from *c.* 1615-20 to the 1630s. Formerly the favourites were Nicolaas (b. 1618) and Albert (b. 1614), but some nowadays prefer Frans (b. 1633), the second son of Rubens's marriage to Helena Fourment. According to L. Burchard and R.-A. d'Hulst the drawing is a study for the child Jesus in *The Return from the Flight into Egypt*, and was made in *c.* 1615-17; this is unproved, but the date would fit in with the use of Albert as a model. A boy with feet in this position occurs in *The Happy Reign*, a painting in the Medici cycle, executed in 1622-25 for the Palais du Luxembourg in Paris and now in the Louvre. J.S. Held, however, believes on stylistic and iconographical grounds that the drawing dates from the 1630s, and considers that the head bears a strong resemblance to that of Rubens's son Frans.

Black and red chalk, heightened with white, 286:210 mm.

Bibl.: K.T. Parker, *Study of a Child's Head and Feet*, in *Old Master Drawings*, IX, 1934-35, pp. 15, 16; *Burchard-d'Hulst, 1956*, p. 74, No. 79; *Held*, p. 142, No. 125; M. Jaffé, *"The Return from the Flight into Egypt" by Peter Paul Rubens*, in *Wadsworth Atheneum Bulletin*, IV, No. 8, Summer 1961, pp. 10-26; *Burchard-d'Hulst, 1963*, pp. 124-6, No. 75.

Prov.: J.F. Gigoux (Paris, 1806-94), who bequeathed it to the city of Besançon.

Musée des Beaux-Arts, Besançon

This sheet comprises studies for *Cupid Begging Jupiter to Consent to his Marriage to Psyche* (Apuleius, *Metamorphoses*, VI: 22), a painting of the period 1610-20, the composition of which is recorded *inter alia* in a drawn copy now at Copenhagen: the latter formerly belonged to Willem Panneels, to whose care Rubens entrusted his studio during his diplomatic journeys to Madrid and London in 1628-30. A canvas (241 : 193 cm) discovered ten years ago and now in the Forbes Magazine Collection in New York is regarded by some art historians as the original painting and by others as an old copy.

The present drawing shows Cupid's head and right arm – in the painting he holds a sheaf of thunderbolts – and Jupiter's right hand.

Black chalk, heightened with white, 314 : 266 mm.

Bibl.:   *Burchard-d'Hulst, 1963*, pp. 190, 191, No. 121; J.R. Martin, *Rubens's 'Jupiter and Cupid': An Exhibition at Princeton*, in *Apollo*, October 1971, pp. 277-9.

Prov.:   The Hon. Mrs. Fitzroy-Newdegate, Arbury Hall, Nuneaton, Warwickshire, England, sold at Christie's, London, 14 March 1952, lot 249, purchased by Colnaghi, London. Acquired by the Museum in 1953.

The National Gallery of Canada, Ottawa

Reversed drawing of a classical marble bust known as *The Dying Alexander*, in the Uffizi, Florence.

Rubens used this study, made *c.* 1615, for the head of St. Stephen in the centre panel of the St. Stephen triptych in the abbey of Saint-Amand-les-Eaux near Valenciennes, now in the Valenciennes Museum.

Formerly sometimes attributed to Van Dyck, this drawing was identified as Rubens's work by J. Koeznetsov. However, this identification is not universally accepted.

This subject, engraved by Paul Pontius, occurs on a sheet of nine heads in a Drawing Book published at Antwerp by Petrus van Avont.

Charcoal(?) and black chalk on grey paper, 340:270 mm.

Bibl.: J. Koeznetsov, Cat. Exh. *Hollandse en Vlaamse tekeningen uit de zeventiende eeuw, Verzameling van de Hermitage, Leningrad, en het Museum Poesjkin, Moskou*, Brussels-Rotterdam-Paris, 1972-73, p. 55, No. 81; Review of this exhibition by E. Haverkamp Begemann in *Master Drawings*, No. 2, 1973, pp. 176-8.

Prov.: Count K. Cobenzl (Vienna, Brussels, 1712-70). Acquired in 1770 by Catherine II.

Print-room, Museum of the Hermitage, Leningrad

Study of trees in a landscape, used by Rubens for his *Boar-Hunt,*
c. 1616, now at Dresden. The drawing is notable for its irresistible
dynamic rhythm as well as the realistic depiction of nature. It contains
no human or animal figures, indicating that it was drawn 'from
life'. Rubens made a separate drawing, from a different angle, of
the dead tree on the right: this is now in the Devonshire Collection
at Chatworth.

Rubens's interest in gnarled, twisted trees is certainly in line with
the North European tradition, but he may also have been stimulated
by sixteenth-century Italian landscapes.

Lower right corner restored. Pen and brown ink over preliminary work in black
chalk, 582:489 mm.

Bibl.: *Rooses*, V, p. 301, No. 1591; E. Michel, *Rubens, sa vie, son œuvre et son temps,*
        Paris, 1900, p. 254; L. Burchard, *Drei Zeichnungen in Dresdner Sammlungen,*
        in *Mitteilungen aus den Sächsischen Kunstsammlungen*, IV, Dresden, 1913, p. 60;
        F. Lugt, *Notes sur Rubens*, in *Gazette des Beaux-Arts*, 1925, II, pp. 193-6;
        Glück-Haberditzl, p. 47, No. 134; G. Glück, *Die Landschaften von P.P. Rubens,*
        Vienna, 1945, pp. 19, 20, 57 (under No. 8); *Lugt, Louvre, Ecole flamande,*
        II, 1949, p. 20, No. 1034; *Held*, p. 145, No. 131; *Burchard-d'Hulst, 1963,*
        pp. 168, 169, No. 104.

Prov.: Confiscated from émigrés at the time of the first French Revolution.

Cabinet des dessins, Musée du Louvre, Paris

A preliminary sketch for *The Descent from the Cross*, formerly in the Capuchin church and now in the Lille Museum, a painting which was not yet delivered on 10 March 1617. The drawing is certainly prior to an oil sketch, also in the Lille Museum. Rubens had already treated this theme in masterly fashion in the centre panel, completed in 1612, of the triptych of the same title in Antwerp cathedral. The drawing has some elements in common with that work, including the diagonal composition and the man holding the shroud between his teeth, a figure that already occurs in *The Washing and Anointing of Christ's Body* in Rotterdam (see No. 133). The twisted pose of the figure of Christ is typical of the period of the drawing.

Pen and brush in reddish brown, 219:158 mm.

Bibl.:   M. Jaffé, *Un chef-d'œuvre mieux connu*, in *L'Œil*, 43-4, Summer 1958, pp. 14-21; *Burchard-d'Hulst, 1963*, pp. 118, 119, No. 71.

Prov.:   Marquis de Robien. Acquired by the Museum at the end of the eighteenth century.

Musée des Beaux-Arts, Rennes

Half-length study 'from life' of a naked man, who is evidently carrying a heavy burden with his hands. L. Burchard connected it with
the figure of St. John receiving the dead body of Christ in *The
Descent from the Cross* (Lille Museum, see No. 144). This identification
is not precluded by the fact that the man in the drawing is naked
while St. John in the painting is clothed. There are other examples
of Rubens using nude studies for clothed figures in his pictures,
e.g. the *Male Nude, Facing Right* in the collection of Her Majesty
the Queen of the Netherlands (see No. 131).

Sheet partially cut down on the right and pasted on to a larger sheet. Black chalk
heightened with white, 280:262 mm.

Bibl.: K.T. Parker, *Catalogue of the Collection of Drawings in the Ashmolean Museum*,
I, Oxford, 1938, pp. 85, 86 (under No. 200); *Burchard*, pp. 57, 58, No.
51; *Burchard-d'Hulst, 1956*, pp. 64, 65, No. 62.

Prov.: J.D. Boehm (Vienna, 1794-1865); E. Wauters (Paris, 1846-1933); F. Koenigs
(Haarlem, 1881-1941). Presented by D.G. van Beuningen to the Boymans
Museum Foundation in 1940.

Boymans-van Beuningen Museum, Rotterdam

This sheet is interesting as it shows how Rubens, in search of a compositional scheme, had no hesitation in drawing over his own lines. He probably began with the head of Christ that is still visible in the lower left-hand corner, and then, being dissatisfied with this, turned the sheet upside-down and started again, most likely with the group in the upper half of the sheet. The lower group, in which Rubens used stronger shadows, is on a smaller scale for lack of space.

This drawing is probably a study for *The Descent from the Cross,* *c.* 1617-18, in the Hermitage at Leningrad; it also shows affinity with the picture of the same title, *c.* 1617, in the Lille Museum. On the verso is a study in pen and brown ink for St. Andrew for the outside of the right-hand panel of *The Miraculous Draught* in Our Lady's church at Mechlin, a triptych painted *c.* 1618-19 for the Mechlin fishmongers' guild.

Pen and brown ink and brown wash, 345 : 233 mm.

Bibl.:   K.T. Parker, *Some Drawings by Rubens and His School in the Collection of Mrs. G.W. Wrangham*, in *Old Master Drawings*, III, 1928, pp. 1, 2; M.V. Dobroklonsky, *Einige Rubenszeichnungen in der Ermitage*, in *Zeitschrift für bildende Kunst*, LXIV, 1930-1, p. 32; K.T. Parker, *Study of a Standing Man*, in *Old Master Drawings*, XI, 1936-37, pp. 50, 51; *Held*, p. 109, No. 42; *Burchard-d'Hulst, 1963*, pp. 160, 161 (under No. 96).

Prov.:   Mrs. G.W. Wrangham; Edward Wrangham; Baskett and Day, art dealers, London.

Mr. and Mrs. Eugene Victor Thaw, New York

Study 'from life' of a nude man, kneeling and seen from behind; the drawing renders not only the posture but the movement of the body. Note the turn of the head and the flexible left foot. The incomplete right leg is repeated in the lower left corner.

This is one of two known studies for the man setting down a large bronze wine-jar in the painting *Abraham and Melchizedek, c.* 1618, Caen Museum: Rubens, however, used the other study, now in the Louvre, Paris.

This figure repeats a motif used earlier by Rubens in *The Adoration of the Magi*, painted in 1609-10 for the Hall of State in the Antwerp City Hall and now in the Prado, Madrid.

Sheet damaged and restored on the left. Black chalk heightened with white, 520:390 mm.

Bibl.: *Burchard-d'Hulst, 1956*, p. 63, No. 60; *Burchard-d'Hulst. 1963*, pp. 153-5, No. 92; Cat. Exh. *Dessins Flamands et Hollandais du dix-septième siècle, Collections Musées de Belgique – Musée Boymans-van Beuningen, Rotterdam – Institut Néerlandais, Paris*, Paris, 1974, pp. 125, 126, No. 93.

Prov.: P.H. Lankrink (London, 1628-92); G. Bellingham Smith, sold at Amsterdam, 5 July 1927, lot 111; F. Koenigs (Haarlem, 1881-1941). Presented by D.G. van Beuningen to the Boymans Museum Foundation in 1940.

Boymans-van Beuningen Museum, Rotterdam

Study 'from life' of a blind man with arms outstretched gropingly. The modelling shadows are lightly drawn, but the cast shadows are rendered by dark hatching, rapidly and forcefully drawn.

Rubens used this drawing for the half-length figure of a blind beggar in *The Miracles of St. Francis Xavier*, a painting executed in 1619-20 for the Jesuit church at Antwerp and intended to adorn the high altar alternately with *The Miracles of St. Ignatius Loyola*. Both pictures are now at Vienna.

Black chalk heightened with white, 280: 417 mm.

Bibl.:   *Rooses*, V, pp. 200, 201, No. 1381; *Glück-Haberditzl*, p. 44, No. 120; *Evers, 1942*, p. 218; *Vlieghe, Saints*, II, p. 32, No. 104d.

Prov.:   Duke Albert von Sachsen-Teschen (Moritzburg by Dresden, and Vienna, 1738-1822).

Graphische Sammlung Albertina, Vienna

ANGEL BEARING A TORCH

Jacobus de Wit (1695-1755) states in his description of the Antwerp **149** churches that the statues above the high altar of the Jesuit church were designed by Rubens: „... de Belden daer boven op synde syn appaert door Rubens geschildert geweest ...". In view of the strong resemblance between this drawing and the statues of angels, which have survived, we may assume that it is in fact a rough sketch for the statues, which were probably carved by Hans van Mildert.

The foundation stone of the Jesuit church was laid in 1615, and in 1621 the church was consecrated by Bishop Jan Malderus. Rubens not only executed paintings for the church but contributed largely to its sculptural decoration, both outside and within.

Drawing irregularly cut out and pasted on a larger sheet. Pen and brown ink over black chalk, grey-brown wash, 196:89 mm. Below, in Rubens's hand, the inscriptions *voeten* and *hooch*. The fragment of a cornice on the right is by another hand.

Bibl.: *Glück-Haberditzl*, p. 46, No. 132; *Bock-Rosenberg*, p. 250, No. 3242; *Burchard-d'Hulst, 1963*, p. 186, under No. 116.

Prov.: Formerly in the archives of the church of St. Charles Borromeo, Antwerp.

Staatliche Museen Preußischer Kulturbesitz, Kupferstichkabinett, Berlin-West

A first, very rough sketch for *The Crucifixion*, also called *Le coup de lance*, which Rubens painted in 1620 for the high altar of the church of Friars Minor at Antwerp and which is now in the city Museum. The dead Christ hangs on the cross between the two thieves. Mary Magdalen stands at his feet with upraised arms, while a Roman soldier pierces his side with a lance. A ladder is propped against the cross of the thief on the right, and a man climbing on it is about to break the thief's legs with a heavy staff. This man is drawn again separately on the extreme right.

On the verso, in pen, is a sketch for the figure of Christ on the cross, and on the right, in outline, another sketch for one of the thieves. Other studies for this *Crucifixion* are known, e.g. that of a *Man Carrying a Ladder* in the Albertina, Vienna (see No. 151).

A narrow strip was later added to the sheet. Pen and brown ink, 206:164 mm.

Bibl.: *Burchard*, p. 50, No. 41; *Burchard-d'Hulst, 1956*, pp. 81, 82, No. 91; *Burchard-d'Hulst, 1963*, pp. 187, 188, No. 118.

Prov.: F.J.O. Boymans (Rotterdam, 1767-1847); bequeathed by him to the city of Rotterdam.

Boymans-van Beuningen Museum, Rotterdam

Study 'from life' of a young man carrying a ladder in a somewhat unusual way, with his head between the rungs. His sleeves are rolled up and he looks towards the spectator.

The drawing is part of the preparatory work for *The Crucifixion (Le coup de lance)* in the Antwerp Museum (see No. 150). The man with the ladder does not appear in the picture itself, but he figures in an oil sketch of the same subject belonging to the Victoria and Albert Museum but exhibited at the National Gallery in London, which some attribute to Rubens and others to Van Dyck.

Slightly browned paper. Black chalk, heightened with white, 342 : 270 mm.

Bibl.: *Schönbrunner-Meder*, VIII, No. 870; T.W. Muchall-Viebrook, *Flemish Drawings of the Seventeenth Century*, London, 1926, p. 28, No. 6; *Held*, pp. 135, 136, No. 99; *Burchard-d'Hulst, 1963*, pp. 189, 190, No. 120.

Prov.: Duke Albert von Sachsen-Teschen (Moritzburg by Dresden, and Vienna, 1738-1822).

Graphische Sammlung Albertina, Vienna

This unforgettable head of a small boy with downcast eyes is drawn with a light and tender hand. Most authors believe it to be a portrait of one of Rubens's sons, like some other drawings of boys' heads in the Albertina; the child's identity is a matter of dispute, but it is generally supposed to be Nicolaas, the son of Rubens and his first wife Isabella Brant. Nicolaas was baptized at St. James's church in Antwerp on 23 March 1618 and died on 28 September 1655.

Rubens used this portrait study for the head of the child Jesus in *Mary, Refuge of Sinners*, a painting in the Kassel Museum.

Red, black and some white chalk; the eyes, mouth and necklet reworked with the pen and Chinese ink; 252:202 mm.

Bibl.: *Rooses*, V, pp. 271, 272, No. 1520; *Schönbrunner-Meder*, IV, No. 435; T.W. Muchall-Viebrook, *Flemish Drawings of the Seventeenth Century*, London, 1926, p. 30, No. 16; *Glück-Haberditzl*, pp. 43, 44, No. 116; E. Kieser, *Rubens' Madonna im Blumenkranz*, in *Münchener Jahrbuch der bildenden Kunst*, 3 Series, I, 1950, p. 222; *Held*, p. 135, No. 98.

Prov.: Duke Albert von Sachsen-Teschen (Moritzburg by Dresden, and Vienna, 1738-1822).

Graphische Sammlung Albertina, Vienna

P.P. Rubens 1788

Costume study for a figure in the portrait of Alatheia Talbot, Countess of Arundel, now in the Alte Pinakothek at Munich. A letter of 17 July 1620 to the Earl of Arundel from one of his agents states that Rubens had just begun work on a portrait of the Countess with her jester, her dog and the dwarf Robin. The Countess had stopped briefly at Antwerp on her way from The Hague to Brussels, and, as Rubens did not have a sufficiently large canvas, he had to confine himself for the time being to sketching the faces, figures and costumes. The painting shows the Countess seated on a terrace in front of four pillars on which a banner is hung with the arms of the Howard family, dukes of Norfolk and earls of Arundel, and the motto *Sola virtus invicta*. Beside her are the jester, the dog and the dwarf Robin with a falcon on his wrist; at the back is Sir Dudley Carleton, English ambassador at The Hague.

Light grey paper, pen and brown ink over red, black and white chalk, 403:258 mm. Notes in Rubens's hand concerning colours and costume materials: *Het Wambuys vermach wesen root sattijn ende de broek root flouweel* (the doublet can be red satin and the breeches red velvet) (above left), *Tannyt flouweel* (tawny velvet) (jacket), *Tannyt flouweel* (tawny velvet) (breeches), *root* (red) (knee), *Geel* (yellow) (stockings), *root* (red) (shoelace), *swart* (black) (shoes) and *Geel voyeringe* (yellow lining of the cloak).

Bibl.: *Rooses*, V, p. 260, No. 1498; *Held*, p. 136, No. 101; *Burchard-d'Hulst, 1963*, pp. 198, 199, No. 127.

Prov.: P. Crozat (Paris, 1665-1740); Count C.G. Tessin (Stockholm, 1695-1770); acquired by the Royal Museum in 1722.

Nationalmuseum, Stockholm

In ancient Rome a small temple was dedicated to Vesta, goddess of the hearth. A flame was kept alight in it by six priestesses known as the Vestals, who were bound by a strict oath to preserve their virginity. Tuccia, one of these, was accused of breaking her oath but proved her innocence by carrying water from the Tiber in a sieve (Pliny, *Nat. Hist.*, XXVIII:3, 12).

In this rapid sketch we see on the left the Pontifex Maximus, who kept a strict watch over the Vestal Virgins, and three other priests; on the right, beside Tuccia, three other Vestals, the centre one pointing to the miracle, and in the foreground the god of the river Tiber, supporting the sieve with one hand and resting his other arm on a jar with water streaming from it.

This subject had previously been treated in Italy and also in the North, by Stradanus among others. Rubens must have been familiar with several versions: it was a popular theme because of its analogy with the Virgin Mary.

E. Kieser rightly connected the present drawing with the Medici cycle (see Nos. 63-67), one reason being that on the verso is a sketch for *The Coming of Age of Louis XIII*, a painting from the same cycle. The Vestal's untarnished honour was an allusion to Marie de' Medici's innocence of the murder of Henry IV. However, Rubens's choice of theme was rejected as it was thought too complicated, and also because it was considered safer to avoid any reference to the murder.

Upper right corner of sheet restored. Pen and brown ink, traces of black chalk, 227:315 mm.

Bibl.: *Rooses*, V, pp. 245-7, Nos. 1474, 1471 (reverse); *Glück-Haberditzl*, p. 50, No. 154; p. 49, No. 147 (reverse); F. Lugt, *Notes sur Rubens*, in *Gazette des Beaux-Arts*, 1925, II, pp. 185-93; *Lugt, Louvre, Ecole flamande, II, 1949*, p. 14, Nos. 1015, 1016 (reverse); E. Kieser, *Die Rubens-Literatur seit 1935*, in *Zeitschrift für Kunstgeschichte*, X, 1941, p. 312; *Burchard-d'Hulst, 1956*, pp. 85, 86, No. 97; *Held*, pp. 114, 115, No. 50; *Burchard-d'Hulst, 1963*, pp. 200-3, No. 129; *Thuillier-Foucart*, pp. 61 (N. 108), 80 (under No. 12).

Prov.: St. Maurice, sold in Paris on 6 February 1786, lot 806, and purchased by Langlier. Confiscated from émigrés at the end of the eighteenth century.

Cabinet des dessins, Musée du Louvre, Paris

It was F. Lugt who identified the subject of this drawing and attributed it to Rubens. The elderly St. Anne, seated in the centre, proudly hands her new-born daughter to Joachim, who takes the child in his hands. A young woman holding a cloth stoops in the left foreground, while four others look on in the background. On the left is the lying-in bed with drawn curtains.

The drawing is not directly connected with any picture by Rubens, and for this and other reasons its dating is doubtful: J.S. Held placed it around 1604-07, F. Lugt around 1612-17. L. Burchard and R.-A. d'Hulst think it may have been drawn for the purpose of the Medici cycle.

Pen and brown ink on grey paper, 254:363 mm.

Bibl.: F. Lugt, *Notes sur Rubens*, in *Gazette des Beaux-Arts*, 1925, II, p. 193; idem, *Les dessins des Ecoles du nord de la collection Dutuit*, Paris, 1927, p. 30, No. 65; *Glück-Haberditzl*, p. 38, No. 76; *Held*, pp. 98, 99, No. 12; *Burchard-d'Hulst*, *1963*, pp. 199, 200, No. 128.

Prov.: Eugène and Auguste Dutuit (Rouen, 1807-86 and 1812-1902). Bequeathed by A. Dutuit to the city of Paris in 1902.

Musée du Petit Palais, Paris

Study 'from life' of a man with Western features wearing Chinese costume, his hands buried in wide sleeves. This is one of a group of five full-length drawings of men in exotic dress: it may be regarded as a largely finished copy by Rubens himself after a sheet in Stockholm, one of the other four.

The inscription in Rubens's hand refers to the Chinese costume and more especially to that worn by Chinese scholars and Jesuit fathers. It reads: "Note that the blackish colour is not peculiar to Chinese scholars but to the fathers of the Society of Jesus, except for the blue galloon which is worn by all. Nor do the Chinese confine themselves to a single colour, but dress in any they please except for yellow, which is reserved for the king." As the Jesuits' principal college was at Antwerp, it is not hard to imagine where Rubens saw such garments or heard them spoken of. Very probably he induced Jesuit fathers to pose for him in Chinese dress.

The drawing may be dated 1622-28, before Rubens's diplomatic journeys to Madrid and London.

Black chalk, heightened with red in the man's features and turquoise in the collar and cuffs; 448:260 mm. Above right, in Rubens's hand: *Nota quod collor pullus non est peculiaris Sinensium litteratis sed Patribus S. Jesu. Exceptis tamen fascijs ceruleis quae ceteris communes sunt. Sinensis porro vestis colore non uno sed quovis colore promiscue utuntur. Et unum reserves flavum scilicet qui proprius est Regis.*

Bibl.:   Miss Clare Stuart Wortley, *Rubens' Drawings of Chinese Costume*, in *Old Master Drawings*, IX, 1934, pp. 40-7; *Burchard-d'Hulst, 1956*, p. 67, under No. 66; *Burchard-d'Hulst, 1963*, pp. 230-2, No. 147.

Prov.:   Lady Sidmouth; Eliza Hobhouse (1842); the Rt. Hon. Henry Hobhouse. *Private collection, U.S.A.*

Portrait of Nicolaas, Rubens's son by his first wife, Isabella Brant. Nicolaas was baptized on 23 March 1618 in St. James's church at Antwerp (see No. 152). He appears to be between seven and nine years old in the drawing, and there is broad agreement that it was executed between 1625 and 1627.

The drawing is decidedly portrait-like; no painting based on it has so far been traced.

Red and black chalk, heightened with white, 292:232 mm.

Bibl.:   *Rooses*, V, p. 273, No. 1524; *Schönbrunner-Meder*, No. 111; *Glück-Haberditzl*, p. 51, No. 163; *Held*, p. 139, No. 109; *Burchard-d'Hulst, 1963*, p. 198, under No. 126.

Prov.:   Duke Albert von Sachsen-Teschen (Moritzburg by Dresden, and Vienna, 1738-1822).

Graphische Sammlung Albertina, Vienna

Rubens drew inspiration more than once from a certain antique bust which was thought in the seventeenth century to represent the Roman statesman, philosopher and poet Seneca, and of which he possessed a marble copy. The bust, seen from the same angle as in this drawing, also appears in the *Group Portrait* painted *c.* 1611-12 and now in the Pitti Palace at Florence, in which Rubens depicted himself, his brother Philip and the humanist Johannes Woverius listening to their tutor Justus Lipsius. It was the latter's aim to bring out the aspects of Seneca's doctrine and moral teaching that could be harmonized with Christianity; he edited, with a commentary, an edition of Seneca's works for which Rubens designed a title-page with a bust of the Roman philosopher.

The present drawing was executed as the model for an engraving by Lucas Vorsterman: one of a series of twelve designed by Rubens after antique marbles or casts thereof, and representing Greek and Roman emperors, commanders and philosophers. Although nine of the engravings bear the date *1638*, it is probable that the edition was planned earlier.

Pen and brown ink and brown wash over black chalk, 257:180 mm.

Bibl.: *Rooses*, V, pp. 14, 15, No. 1218; *Goris-Held*, p. 43, No. 111; *Burchard-d'Hulst, 1956*, pp. 87, 88 (under No. 99); Cat. Exh. *Drawings and Oil Sketches by Rubens from American Collections*, Cambridge-New York, 1956, p. 18, No. 13.

Prov.: Collection of the Earl of Warwick.

The Metropolitan Museum of Art, Robert Lehman Collection, New York

The Madonna is enthroned on a pedestal. The child Jesus on her lap bends down towards St. Catherine, who stands at the Virgin's feet with the little St. John. Some putti are standing to the right of the pedestal. The central group thus formed is surrounded by saints. Mary is turned slightly to the left, where St. Peter and two groups of female saints look up towards her. In the foreground on the left are St. Sebastian and St. George, and on the right St. Augustine. The composition is such that the eye is led to follow it in a circular movement.

In the upper half of the verso are several studies of the Virgin and Child, separately and together. Like the subsequent drawing on the recto they are studies for *The Madonna with Saints*, painted in 1628 for the high altar of the Augustinian church at Antwerp. Rubens took great care over this picture, for which he also made oil sketches both for the composition as a whole and for individual figures (see Nos. 79, 80).

In the lower half of the verso are studies for the *Landscape with St. George*, now in Buckingham Palace, painted in 1629-30 when Rubens was ambassador to the English court.

Sheet folded in two. Tip of the brush in brown ink and brown wash over preliminary work in black chalk, 561 : 412 mm.

Bibl.: F. Lugt, *Notes sur Rubens*, in *Gazette des Beaux-Arts*, 1925, II, p. 199 e.a.; *Glück-Haberditzl*, p. 53, No. 172; F. Grossmann, *Notes on Some Dutch and Flemish Paintings at Rotterdam*, in *The Burlington Magazine*, XCVII, 1955, pp. 335-8; *Burchard-d'Hulst, 1956*, pp. 92, 93, No. 108; *Held*, p. 117, No. 53; *Burchard-d'Hulst, 1963*, pp. 225-7, No. 145.

Prov.: Count C.G. Tessin (Stockholm, 1695-1770). Acquired by the Royal Museum in 1773.

Nationalmuseum, Stockholm

The victorious hero approaches, from the right, a naked woman standing in the centre of the drawing, who represents Opportunity *(Occasio)*. To her left, another woman is seated on a globe with a rudder beside her (good counsel or secular government); a putto offers her fruit. The hero, with a lion at his feet, is accompanied by Minerva, whose shield is on his arm, and who places in his grasp the long, loosened hair of the Opportunity figure. Chronos (Time) – alluding to the suitability of the moment for concluding peace – hovers in the air with an owl, Minerva's attribute, beside him, together with genii bearing emblems of fame and conquest.

When Rubens had finished the Medici cycle for the Palais du Luxembourg in Paris (see p. 151), he was required to paint a further series of pictures showing the life and achievements of King Henry IV of France. Among these was to be a painting of *Henry IV Seizing the Opportunity to Make Peace*, celebrating the treaty of Vervins concluded with Spain in 1598, and forming a pendant to *The Battle of Coutras*. The ambitious undertaking on which Rubens was active from 1627 to 1631 was, however, discontinued owing to political circumstances in France. Subsequently Rubens used the allegory in the present drawing for a painting which is now lost.

At the top, a strip of paper added by Rubens himself. Black chalk, water-colour and body-colour, 383:477 mm.

Bibl.: *Rooses*, V, p. 246, No. 1472; *Rubens-Bulletijn*, V, 1897, pp. 80-2; Cat. *Nachlass Miethke*, sold in Vienna, Dorotheum, 12 Juny 1933, lot 69; *Burchard-d'Hulst, 1956*, pp. 99, 100, No. 118; *Burchard-d'Hulst, 1963*, pp. 258-60, No. 168.

Prov.: Probably in the estate of E. Jabach (Paris, 1607/10-95); Gottfried Winkler, Leipzig; Hofrat Rochlitz, Leipzig; presented to the Weimar Museum, 1839.

Staatliche Kunstsammlungen, Weimar

Thomas Howard, second Earl of Arundel, is depicted in half-length, his head turned towards the spectator. He is in armour, and his outstretched arm rests on a staff. A drapery is sketched above, and a helmet below.

The drawing was made during Rubens's stay in London in 1629-30. A letter from London to Pierre Dupuy, dated 8 August 1629, mentions that he had seen the Arundel collections, and the drawing was probably made during his visit to Arundel House. It shows the Earl at forty-five years of age, and is a study for the portrait now in the Isabella Stewart Gardner Museum in Boston. The sketch-like technique indicates that it was done rapidly and from life. See No. 82.

Brush and brown and black ink, heightened with white and with touches of red, 464 : 356 mm.

Bibl.: *Glück-Haberditzl*, p. 54, No. 178; G. Glück, *Rubens as a Portrait Painter*, in *The Burlington Magazine*, LXXVI, 1940, p. 174; *Burchard-d'Hulst, 1963*, pp. 263, 264, No. 170; E. Haverkamp Begemann, Standish D. Lawder and Charles W. Talbot Jr., *Drawings from the Clark Art Institute*, New Haven-London, 1964, pp. 28, 29, No. 22.

Prov.: G.H. (unidentified collector of the first half of the eighteenth century, perhaps Guillaume Hubert); Jonathan Richardson Sr. (London, 1665-1745), sold in London, 22 January 1747; Thomas Hudson (London, 1701-79), sold in London, 24 March 1779, lot 69 (to Lord Selsey); Lord Selsey, sold at Sotheby's, London, 1872 (to Roupell); Robert L. Roupell (London, 1798-1886), sold at Christie's, London, 12-14 July 1887, lot 1120; private collection, London (1926).

The Stirling and Francine Clark Art Institute, Williamstown, Massachusetts

This masterly study 'from life' was used for at least three paintings of the same subject, *A Maid and a Youth in a Pantry*, the still life being painted in each case by Frans Snijders (1579-1657). The pictures belong respectively to the collections of the Marquess of Bute, the Marquis du Parc Locmaria and the late Paul Getty. In each of them the figure of the girl varies in detail from the drawing, as her clothing and pose were adapted to her occupation in the picture and to compositional needs. There is disagreement as to who executed this figure in the three paintings. The drawing must have been made in the late twenties or early thirties.

Black and red chalk, heightened with white chalk, 472:301 mm.

Bibl.:   *Glück-Haberditzl*, p. 58, Nr. 212; *Glück*, pp. 178-87; *Held*, p. 141, No. 116; *Burchard-d'Hulst, 1963*, pp. 270-2, No. 176; M. Jaffé, *Rubens and Snijders, a fruitful Partnership*, in *Apollo*, XCIII, March 1971, p. 184 e.a., p. 193; Cat. Exh. *Vlaamse tekeningen uit de zeventiende eeuw*, London-Paris-Bern-Brussels, 1972, pp. 125-7, No. 84.

Prov.:   W. Oudenaarden, sold at Haarlem on 1 November 1796; W.Ph. Kops, Haarlem, sold at Amsterdam on 14 March 1808; Jacob de Vos Jbzn (Amsterdam, 1803-82), sold at Amsterdam on 2 May 1883, lot 450; P. Langerhuizen Lzn, sold at Amsterdam on 19 April 1919 from lot 914, and purchased by F. Lugt.

Fondation Custodia (coll. F. Lugt), Institut Néerlandais, Paris

Previously regarded as a copy and afterwards as 'School of Rubens', this was recognized by F. Lugt as a drawing by Rubens's own hand, though he did not place it among the master's best works. The figure is repeated almost literally in *Diana and Callisto*, Madrid, and *Diana and her Nymphs Surprised by Satyrs*, Berlin, while the upper part is strongly reminiscent of the half-naked Helena Fourment in *The Fur Wrap*, Vienna – all three paintings dating from Rubens's last years. However, Lugt believed that the drawing should be dated twenty or twenty-five years earlier, and he pointed out that Rubens often used older studies for his paintings. He considered the resemblance to Helena Fourment to be irrelevant to the dating, as the painter's second wife embodied an ideal of physical beauty that recurs throughout his work. H.G. Evers regards the drawing as a study for *The Fur Wrap*.

Red and black chalk, somewhat heightened with white, 463 : 282 mm.

Bibl.: E. Michel, *Rubens, sa vie, son œuvre et son temps*, Paris, 1900, Pl. XI; *Evers, 1942*, pp. 454, 457; *Lugt, Louvre, Ecole flamande, II, 1949*, pp. 19, 20, No. 1032.

Prov.: Unknown.

Cabinet des dessins, Musée du Louvre, Paris

A young man, seen full-face, embraces a young woman. He wears a doublet with slashed sleeves and a broad-brimmed hat. The woman's figure is merely outlined. According to L. Burchard and R.-A. d'Hulst this is a study for the large pen-and-ink model executed by Rubens for a woodcut to be engraved by Christoffel Jegher (1596-1652/5). This model (48:142 cm), now in the Metropolitan Museum of Art in New York, probably dates from *c.* 1632-33 and is based on *The Garden of Love*, a painting in the collection of James Rothschild, Waddesdon Manor, Buckinghamshire. The reason why the woman is only drawn in outline is probably that Rubens had already made the detailed study of a young woman now in the Städelsches Kunstinstitut at Frankfort am Main, from which he incorporated various details in the large model. The young couple recur in a somewhat different pose in the other painting *The Garden of Love*, Prado, Madrid (see No. 91). Some authors believe that the present drawing was a preparatory study for that painting.

Rubens drew other studies from life as a preparation for the large model in New York (see Nos. 165, 166).

Black and red chalk, heightened with white, on grey paper, 325:301 mm.

Bibl.: *Rooses*, V, pp. 250, 251 (No. 1482), 252 (No. 1486); *Glück-Haberditzl*, p. 56, No. 198; *Burchard-d'Hulst, 1956*, pp. 101, 102, No. 122; *Held*, p. 142, No. 120; *Burchard-d'Hulst, 1963*, pp. 282, 283, No. 181.

Prov.: T. Hudson (London, 1701-79)?; Sir Thomas Lawrence (London, 1769-1830); King William II of the Netherlands, sold from his estate in 1850 and bought by C.J. Fodor (Amsterdam, d. 1860). Bequeathed by C.J. Fodor to the City of Amsterdam.

Historisch Museum, C.J. Fodor collection, Amsterdam

9

Study 'from life' of a young woman in luxurious clothes, seated on the ground. A preliminary study for *The Garden of Love*, Metropolitan Museum of Art, New York, a large model executed by Rubens for a woodcut by Christoffel Jegher (see under No. 164). In the New York drawing she rests her right arm on the knees of a woman sitting beside her, while the hand of another companion rests on her left arm.

This seated young woman recurs, though in a different pose, in the painting *The Garden of Love*, Prado, Madrid (see No. 91) and in the painting of the same title owned by James Rothschild, Waddesdon Manor, Buckinghamshire. Some authors believe that the present drawing was a preparatory study for the Madrid version.

Sheet restored, below right. Black and red chalk, heightened with white, 424:500 mm.

Bibl.:   *Glück-Haberditzl*, p. 57, No. 200; *Bock-Rosenberg*, p. 252, No. 4003; *Burchard-d'Hulst, 1956*, p. 102, No. 123; *Burchard-d'Hulst, 1963*, pp. 285, 286, No. 183.

Prov.:   J. Richardson Jr. (London, 1694-1771); Earl of Aylesford (London and Packington Hall, Warwickshire, 1786-1859), sold in London, 18 July 1893, lot 271. Acquired in 1893.

Staatliche Museen Preußischer Kulturbesitz, Kupferstichkabinett, Berlin-West

A young gentleman in a rich doublet and puff-breeches, wearing a broad-brimmed hat and with a cloak over his shoulder, stretches out his right hand; the left hand rests on the pommel of his sword, the tip of which is hidden under the cloak.

The attitude and movement of this study 'from life' answer to the purpose for which it was drawn: in the two painted versions of *The Garden of Love*, one in the Prado, Madrid (see No. 91), and the other in the collection of James Rothschild, Waddesdon Manor, Buckinghamshire, the young man descends a flight of steps and supports a lady on his right arm. This figure does not appear in the large model for Christoffel Jegher's woodcut (see under No. 164).

Black and red chalk, heightened with white, on light brown paper, 561:415 mm.

Bibl.:   *Glück-Haberditzl*, p. 57, No. 205; *Glück*, pp. 105-7; *Burchard-d'Hulst, 1956*, pp. 102, 103, No. 124; *Held*, p. 142, No. 119.

Prov.:   T. Hudson (London, 1701-79)?; Sir Thomas Lawrence (London, 1769-1830); King William II of the Netherlands, sold from his estate in 1850 and bought by C.J. Fodor (Amsterdam, d. 1860). Bequeathed by C.J. Fodor to the City of Amsterdam.

Historisch Museum, C.J. Fodor collection, Amsterdam

Study 'from life' of an unidentified young woman, seen frontally and half-length. Her head is turned slightly to the right and downwards, and her hands are crossed in her lap; her gaze is reflective, and her whole attitude is one of calm recollection.

This fine study, dating from 1630-35, has been connected with *The Mystic Marriage of St. Catherine*, 1633, previously in the Augustinian church at Mechlin and now in the Toledo Museum of Art, Ohio, and also with *St. Ildefonso Receiving a Chasuble from the Virgin in the Presence of the Archdukes Albert and Isabella*, 1630-32, painted for Saint-Jacques-sur-le-Coudenberg in Brussels and now in the Kunsthistorisches Museum, Vienna. However, the young woman does not occur literally in either of these pictures (see No. 90).

Upper corners slightly damaged. Red and black chalk heightened with white, 473 : 354 mm.

Bibl.: *Glück-Haberditzl*, p. 58, No. 207; J. Jacob, *A 'Holy Family' and other related Pictures by Peter Paul Rubens*, in *Jaarboek Koninklijk Museum voor Schone Kunsten, Antwerpen*, 1954-60, pp. 15, 16; *Held*, p. 139, No. 110; *Burchard-d'Hulst, 1963*, pp. 267-9, No. 174.

Prov.: P.H. Lankrink (London, 1627-92); I.W. Böhler, Lucerne; F. Koenigs (Haarlem, 1881-1941), who bought Böhler's collection in 1929. Presented to the Boymans Museum Foundation by D.G. van Beuningen in 1940.

Boymans-van Beuningen Museum, Rotterdam

In an undulating wooded landscape the Virgin sits at the foot of a tree, her face towards the spectator, with the sleeping child Jesus on her lap. Beside them are the infant St. John and a cherub playing with a lamb, while a third boy with a finger to his lips points towards the child Jesus and warns them not to make a noise. In the middle distance are the grazing donkey and St. Joseph asleep at the foot of a tree.

This careful drawing of 1632-35 is a model for a woodcut by Christoffel Jegher (1596-1652/5). The lines are drawn deliberately and clearly so that the engraver can follow the model accurately. Several proofs of the woodcut have survived: four in the Rijksprentenkabinet at Amsterdam, two in the Bibliothèque Nationale in Paris and one in the Antwerp Museum. All were reworked by Rubens, who in each case stopped out some parts in white.

Pen and brown ink and brown wash over preliminary work in black chalk. Some parts heightened with white and with lightly tinted body-colour, 465:605 mm.

Bibl.: *Burchard-d'Hulst, 1956*, pp. 105, 106, No. 129; *Held*, p. 155, under No. 155; *Burchard-d'Hulst, 1963*, pp. 274-8, No. 179; Mary L. Myers, *Rubens and the Woodcuts of Christoffel Jegher*, in *The Metropolitan Museum of Art Bulletin*, XXV, No. 1, 1966, pp. 7-23.

Prov.: P.J. Mariette (Paris, 1694-1774); Print-Room of King Stanislaw August Poniatowski of Poland (1764-95). Acquired by Count Athanasius Raczyński in 1916. In the Museum at Poznań since 1903.

National Museum, Poznań, Poland

Hercules, brandishing his club, and Minerva with her helmet and shield are repelling Mars, god of war. Mars, in armour, drags a woman by the hair and threatens her with his sword, while a child clings to her. The ground is strewn with dead bodies. Mars's foot rests on a figure lying beside the barrel of a broken gun; a woman collapses holding a musical instrument. In the distance on the right can be seen the burning ruins of a city. In the air, between the heads of Minerva and Mars, is Jupiter's eagle with a thunderbolt in its claws; two Furies hover to the right of Mars.

The theme of war and peace was close to Rubens's heart: he expressed his longing for peace and his deep hatred of war in many allegorical compositions, including this brilliant drawing from the Louvre, dating from *c.* 1635. A corresponding painting is not known.

The figure of Hercules is based on the *Borghese Warrior*, an antique sculpture in the Louvre. In the Boymans-van Beuningen Museum at Rotterdam there is an oil sketch on panel representing the figures of Minerva and Mars; this has been cut down on the left, so that originally it probably comprised Hercules also, and was thus closely connected with the drawing in the Louvre.

Oil (and body-colour?) over preliminary work in black chalk, 370:539 mm.

Bibl.: *Smith, Catalogue Raisonné*, II, p. 129, No. 432; *Idem*, Suppl., p. 278, No. 120; *Reiset*, No. 552; *Rooses*, V, pp. 247, 248, No. 1475; *Idem*, IV, pp. 46, 47, No. 826; *Glück-Haberditzl*, p. 54, No. 182; *Lugt, Louvre, Ecole flamande, II, 1949*, p. 14, No. 1014; Cat. Exh. *Rotterdam, 1953-54*, p. 89, under No. 79; *Burchard-d'Hulst, 1956*, p. 97, No. 115; *Held*, p. 124, No. 66; *Burchard-d'Hulst, 1963*, pp. 260-3, No. 169.

Prov.: Formerly in the possession of the kings of France.

Cabinet des dessins, Musée du Louvre, Paris

In the foreground is a brook that disappears in the middle distance on the right, where it is bordered by willows. Further off are some slender trees behind a weir and a wooden fence, and in the remoter distance are meadows surrounded by woods.

This landscape drawing of *c.* 1635 cannot be related to any painting by Rubens. Although it has traditionally been ascribed to him, critics are not unanimous on this point. The first to attribute it to Rubens in the twentieth century was M.V. Dobroklonsky.

Upper corners cut off; traces of a vertical fold in the middle. Body-colour and tempera over black chalk, 435 : 590 mm.

Bibl.: M.V. Dobroklonsky, *Einige Rubens Zeichnungen in der Eremitage*, in *Zeitschrift für bildende Kunst*, 1930-31, pp. 36, 37; *Burchard-d'Hulst, 1956*, Suppl. p. 9, No. 138a; *Held*, p. 147, under No. 136; *Burchard-d'Hulst, 1963*, pp. 331, 332, No. 208; J. Koeznetsow, Cat. Exh. *Hollandse en Vlaamse tekeningen uit de zeventiende eeuw, Verzameling van de Hermitage, Leningrad, en het Museum Poesjkin, Moskou*, Brussels-Rotterdam-Paris, 1972-73, pp. 58, 59, No. 85.

Prov.: Count Karl Cobenzl (Vienna, Brussels, 1712-70). Acquired by Catherine II in 1770.

Print-room, Museum of the Hermitage, Leningrad

A path starts from the left, runs between a fence and a parapet over a narrow bridge and leads towards a forest of tall trees. The brook flowing under the bridge is bordered with willows.

P. Buschmann suggested that this drawing of *c.* 1635 represented a locality near the Château de Steen, Rubens's country house at Elewijt, between Vilvoorde and Mechlin, where he often stayed during his last years. This is of course possible, but cannot be proved.

Black chalk with touches of red chalk and white body-colour, 383 : 499 mm.

Bibl.: P. Buschmann, *Rubens en Van Dyck in het Ashmolean Museum*, in *Onze Kunst*, XXIX, 1916, pp. 42, 43; *Glück-Haberditzl*, p. 52, No. 170; K.T. Parker, *Catalogue of the Collection of Drawings in the Ashmolean Museum*, I, Oxford, 1938, p. 86, No. 201; *Burchard-d'Hulst, 1956*, pp. 111, 112, No. 138; *Held*, p. 147, No. 137; *Burchard-d'Hulst, 1963*, pp. 330, 331, No. 207.

Prov.: P.H. Lankrink (London, 1628-92); Chambers Hall (Southampton and London, 1786-1855), who bequeathed it to Oxford University.

The Ashmolean Museum, Oxford

Three richly-clad young women hold one another by the arms and shoulders, while three putti tug at their clothes as if to draw them away. A fourth putto hovers in the air, holding a wreath over the head of the woman in the centre. Above on the right is another female figure rapidly sketched in outline. The subject of the scene is not clear. Perhaps the central figure is Psyche, and the putti, symbols of love and of Psyche's lover Cupid, are trying to separate her from her sisters and lead her to him.

A small painting in grey by Rubens, now owned by the City of Milan, shows the same composition as this late drawing and is probably based on it. There is also an anonymous seventeenth-century engraving of the same composition, but reversed.

On the verso is a rapid sketch, in black and red chalk and brown wash, of a group of three naked young women, one of whom is repeated on the right-hand side. The composition of this group is based on Rubens's *Three Graces*, *c.* 1625, in the Vienna Academy, and is closest to that of the painting of the same title in the Prado, Madrid, which dates from *c.* 1636-38.

Sheet damaged on the left. Black and red chalk, and brown wash, 280:250 mm.

Bibl.: *Burchard-d'Hulst, 1956*, p. 116, No. 144; *Burchard-d'Hulst, 1963*, p. 327, No. 205.

Prov.: Collection of the Association of Friends of Learning, Warsaw, 1800-32. In the University Library since 1923.

Print-room of the University Library, Warsaw

This self-portrait, showing Rubens in three-quarter profile with his face towards the spectator, was drawn towards the end of his life as a study for the *Self-Portrait* of *c.* 1638-40 in the Kunsthistorisches Museum, Vienna. The drawing, remarkable for its simplicity and veracity, differs somewhat from the painting, in which the artist is seen in front of an architectural décor and with his left hand on the hilt of his sword. Rubens was over sixty and, though marked by years and ill-health, depicted himself in a stylish, proud and dignified attitude.

The sheet has suffered from exposure to light. It is also marked by brown spots where the ink has penetrated from some rapid sketches made on the back. Black chalk, heightened with white in places, 461 : 287 mm.

Bibl.: *Reiset*, No. 555; *Rooses*, V, pp. 276, 277, No. 1530; *Glück-Haberditzl*, p. 62, No. 235; *Lugt, Louvre, École flamande, II, 1949*, pp. 14, 15, No. 1017; *Held*, p. 143, No. 123; *Burchard-d'Hulst, 1963*, pp. 323-5, No. 202.

Prov.: J. Richardson Sr. (London, 1665-1745); T. Hudson (London, 1701-79); John Barnard (London, d. 1784). Confiscated from French émigrés at the end of the eighteenth century.

Cabinet des dessins, Musée du Louvre, Paris

Sources of photographs:

The photographs of the works have graciously been provided by the owners or by scientific institutes. All rights of reproduction are reserved and subject to permission.

INDEX OF COLLECTIONS

Printed in Belgium / Drukkerij Excelsior, Antwerp